CH00419592

# The Dream of the Mind

## Alex Ehrlich

Copyright © 2020 Alex Ehrlich Publishing

Amazon KDP ISBN 9798683910365

All Rights Reserved.

This book is the sole intellectual property of the author and any reproduction in part or in whole is prohibited without express permission of the author, except by a reviewer who may quote brief passages in a review.

1

"I fully intend to explain to you the underlying nature of our reality depicted in a literal manner never delineated with this accuracy, and also, I intend to explain what *exactly* is our mind, and how our identification with our thoughts and experience prevents our awareness of that underlying nature."

**"IF YOU WANT TO FIND THE SECRETS OF THE UNIVERSE, THINK IN TERMS OF ENERGY, FREQUENCY, AND VIBRATION"**

**NICOLA TESLA**

**The Dream of the Mind.**

# INTRODUCTION

This book is about you.

For people who hunger to understand the human mind and its complexities, this book will be hard to put down. The metaphysics that underlie physical reality and the mysticism that humans produce to explain it are my central theme.

The mystical principle of that which 'is' has been sought for millennia and has divided people into myriad groups, religions, sects, and ideology. It has divided tribes and nations. What people label as divine has done more to create division among people than any other human issue. With this book I intend to resolve that problem. There are links in the footnotes to videos and information to illuminate my points – Please watch them.

This book is a straightforward treatise on actual reality versus conceived reality and how we have been taught to understand it. I do my best to keep your mind from conceptual frameworks that we are used to. The mind ALWAYS wants our reality to fit the traditional, conventional, popular, and contemporary frameworks. The mind craves more information, and less is better which is why allegory, metaphor, motif, and archetypal symbolism have always been the medium for delivering this information.

Carl Jung said this: *"The underlying primary psychic reality is so inconceivably complex that it can be grasped only at the farthest reach of intuition, and then but very dimly. That is why it needs symbols."*[1]

I will be talking about allegory, metaphysics, quantum physics, dreams and dreaming, sound and vibration and the mind – specifically, what your

---

1   Carl Gustav Jung, Practice of Psychotherapy, P. 159

# Wake Up!

mind is, where it is, and how the mind works – and sometimes doesn't work too well at all (what I call 'mind vomit'). I will talk about life situations that demonstrate how this all intertwines.

I try my best to keep this as simple as possible because this book is for everyone. This information is very difficult to convey to people, which is why people throughout history have tried to explain this – but always have come up short. You will learn why they have failed. I have the advantage of current technology and understanding of scientific principles that weren't available before.

I have tried my best to isolate the problem of conceptual reality and explain it in as few pages as possible. The biggest obstacle to understanding what underlies all reality is the mind. The mind is an illusion that demands to be real, and for the mind to be real it must always find errors in our logic, epistemology, and every conceivable angle of argumentation.

When you go to court there are always 2 or more lawyers because there are always opposing arguments. The mind wants to exploit this system of opposing arguments in order to perpetuate a paradox.

Therefore, it's paramount to use as few pages as possible. The mind wants to go off tangentially which only makes things confusing. I succeeded in keeping this under 200 pages – which was my goal!

Have fun with this!

**The Dream of the Mind.**

# *In the Beginning...*

Thus starts an allegorical version of the 'God' story that has been reiterated in all of the world's religions. The underlying message in all these teachings is the same. This message attempts to tell us over and over the same thing in variations of allegory and metaphor. The reason for the differences are due to geography, culture, tradition, competition, and dominance between all the various cultures and traditions, and the fact that different people apply these stories in their own lives in different ways, and therefore, one allegory doesn't work for all people. But, regardless of the metaphors and allegories used, we don't get it – or, for the most part, we *can't* get it. There are a few people who know the reality, or who are close to knowing it, and there are very many who *think* they know it, but most everyone is stuck in what isn't real, and "real" being the root of "real"ity – if they are stuck in what isn't real, then it only follows that they are not connected to the true reality, and this is why our world is dying.

These teachings in all the different religions are road maps to the same underlying truth of our true nature. They are always conveyed to us in allegorical/metaphorical form because of the tacit nature of the underlying reality. It's impossible for the human mind to understand in human terms what underlies that which we call reality while we are in physical form; the true underlying reality (*Oneness*) can only be intuited, but **never** can it be **understood** by the mind. If it were possible to explain in human words the divine then we would all be enlightened, and Jesus, Krishna, and Buddha, among others, would not be well known, they would only be regular people who knew no more than the rest of us; the Bible would not

5

be necessary, nor the Bhagavad Gita, nor the Shiva Sutras, nor the Upanishads, nor the Koran, nor the Torah, nor the many Buddhist texts, nor any other religious exegesis. Many of them focus more on allegory, while others more on practices that are intended to lessen our attachment to the mind, some use both, but regardless, the underlying reality – that which we label as the 'divine' – cannot be understood in human terms, by our mind.

It is intuition that whispers to us that, below the surface, there is more to this existence than we can see or fathom. We know it's there because of intuition, but intuition won't get us there alone. Something greater must happen. There must be an experience that transcends the mind.

At the other end of the spectrum, every few thousand years, it *seems* to be that there is a person born who moves from the underlying still, clear, calm pool of pure *Oneness* into the physical form seamlessly, and their mind remains secondary, and they do not identify with its dream. If true, this type of transition is extremely rare. There are writings that support this, but I have never met such a person, or seen any evidence of this besides writings that are somewhat compelling. It's also quite possible that those who were considered awakened from the time of birth became aware during early adolescence, and not from the moment of birth. There is no way to know for sure. It would be a little bit hard to ask an infant or toddler questions about that.

This book is about our determination to find and attune ourselves with that higher power, and the metaphysics that underlie what we as humans consider reality, which include the tacit message that has many times been handed us in allegorical and metaphorical form, that humans have – throughout history – misinterpreted into distorted versions for the benefit

# The Dream of the Mind.

of our ego, and our ego's craving for power, and life everlasting.

Along with talking about the metaphysical nuts and bolts of the mystical message, this book will also cover a few of those stories, allegories, and metaphors that humans have created to direct our attention to that truth that lies within each and every one of us – and all physical matter. I can never prove anything that I am about to tell you with regard to the metaphysics underlying our physical world, but you need not take my word for it, you need only look to the allegories that we have deliberately created for eons. Humanity has fervently and quite deliberately created road-maps, signposts, and arrows pointing us to the underlying truth that cannot be seen or understood by the mind. We have been for thousands of years working feverishly, with great passion, usually unwittingly, to wake up while in our bodies, therefore it is important to talk about some of these allegories, and explain how they are intended to operate in our lives. In this book I can't go into long explanations of allegory, nor can I cover too many allegories, nor can I go on and on with information, because that would be diametrically opposed to the purpose of this book. The mind wants more and more and more information – not less, and to **Wake Up**, we need less, not more.

Allegory is very important because we use it to illustrate those concepts and ideas where words fail. Sort of like drawing a picture rather than using words. Most folks are more familiar with analogy than allegory, but they are very similar. Both are comparisons, but allegory is a story, such as the story of the 'Tortoise and the Hare,' which illustrates the concept of: 'Slow and Steady is better than Fast and Careless,' or 'The 3 Little Pigs,' which illustrates: 'Build your house from stone and on solid ground,' while analogy is a more basic comparison usually expressed in a single sentence or paragraph, such as: "Her voice was music to my ears," or "March came in like a lion, and went out like a lamb."

The underlying reality cannot be explained with words so allegories of the *transcendent* type have been used to convey to us this information. Trouble is that allegory isn't often recognized, and even more often not correctly interpreted by most people. Not all allegory is of the transcendent type, most metaphor and allegory convey simple life lessons such as with The Hare and the Tortoise, or Beauty and the Beast, but the more important allegories are of the transcending movement of our consciousness from the outer vision to the inner vision. My favorite example of the transcendent allegory is 'The Wizard of Oz.'

There are simple allegories and there are complex allegories. There is no reason for a writer to make his/her allegory complex when the purpose of allegory is to try to convey a simple truth but to make things complex is the nature of the mind. The mind wants to be complex because complexity makes the mind appear sophisticated, and the propensity of the human mind is to appear sophisticated. The mind wants to $$*$hine*$$. The smarter a person the more their mind wants others to recognize its ability to conceptualize incredibly complex concepts and with regard to creating allegory, to the point that the allegory no longer holds true to form – the allegory becomes overly tangential, and begs interpretation, or the more likely outcome: 'misinterpretation.' It's nice to write a complex story with twists and turns, but when it comes to allegory – simple is better. People have a hard enough time with the simple allegories, but writers who have great intellect want the world to see how clever they are so they write incredible stories with complex allegory, metaphor, and archetype, such as the work of James Joyce, especially 'Finnegans Wake,' or Franz Kafka's books – interesting books to read, but the more complex

# The Dream of the Mind.

they get, the more complex the analysis, and the more limited the readership. The Biblical allegory can be tedious as well. The more complex allegories may be intellectually stimulating and intriguing, but not good at all for helping the average person understand whatever lesson is being exemplified.

I want this book to be useful to every person. Other than a few five-dollar words here and there, I try to remain colloquial – perhaps it's a bit intellectual, but not overly so. I think that the subject matter is intellectually steeped; certainly tacit, can't remove those qualities from it, although I don't think that those basic stories that were handed down from generation to generation were meant to be difficult. With that said, I don't think there will be so many five-dollar words that you are overburdened to look them up.

My purpose in talking about allegory isn't to prove anything – it is to simply show how purposefully, and with great effort, humans have been working to Wake Up to who and what we really are. I am not trying to prove that all of the allegories we have written were correct, or ideal, or suitable. I only mean to show how by looking at these allegories you can see that we intuitively know the underlying truth of who and what we are, but the mind cannot grasp it, and drags us down with its insistence that it is independent, is an individual, and that it will exist eternally in spirit as a *soul*. Fortunately, that which underlies all that exists is way ahead of the mind and has skirted around the mind, and through our intuition has – sort-of – tricked the mind into creating allegorical and archetypal breadcrumb trails helping us to find our way back to awareness of that which underlies all of that which exists. That's what allegory, archetypal stories and images are: they are indications and representations of what we already know. And, not just the intellectuals, but all of us can benefit from this.

Most all of the stories that humans create – in one way or another – incorporate an element of becoming – of becoming more than we are – of becoming our own hero, and perhaps even, the hero that transcends the mind. Even stories that don't seem allegorical, or are not intended to be allegory almost always incorporate these elements in one way or another. We use stories to show us the light as well as the dark side of being human. We like to measure our progress on the road of transcendence, and/or the moving away from it – going into darkness. We want to be the hero, but we must have the dark stories with which to contrast being the hero with becoming the villain. So, we write to tell ourselves and remind ourselves, of how our relationship with the 'hero' is either growing or withering. We read these stories about characters that we see as separate from us, just stories we think, but deep down we aspire to be like these hero characters and to understand and align ourselves with their ethical and moral teachings. This effort on the part of humanity to awaken ourselves leaks out of us like a sieve into the stories we tell whether they are in book form, movie form, or oral.

We also read dark stories with an eye toward where we want to avoid going – even though we don't necessarily give this much thought as moral teaching, but subconsciously that's exactly what we are doing. We also need to know and understand our shadow side and to give it expression – because it will find its own expression if we don't. If a person can't give expression to a shadow aspect of him or herself, or if that person doesn't know how to allow the shadow to express itself in their life, then that shadow aspect will find a way to manifest in their life one way or another

# The Dream of the Mind.

– and it may very well manifest in a way that is not beneficial, and/or in a destructive way.

There are people who deliberately do the opposite and purposefully align themselves with the dark side of human nature, which while it may be intriguing and suspenseful, it's loaded with stress and foreboding and not just stress for the individual, but it leaks out and touches all of us – something I will talk about later.

Throughout this book, I will emphasize the necessity of accepting as a part of us both the light and dark sides of who we are for without doing so one cannot awaken. One cannot reject any part of either side, nor align themselves with one side more than the other. We may seek to keep ourselves in the light, but we must also give the dark side its due, and if we find ourselves living in shadows we mustn't turn off the light to make the shadows disappear.


Existence for human life on the Earth is dependent on our waking up. Life on this planet will soon experience a rather abrupt upheaval if we don't make substantial effort to Wake Up – not only substantial *effort* but also substantial *progress*. Arguments might be made that we really need to clean things up, or change this, or change that if we are to save this planet, but any necessary changes will happen in and of themselves – automatically – if we Wake Up, ...so the primary goal is to Wake Up. Without Waking Up cleaning up our planet *may* happen to some degree, but only enough to slow down our demise – it wouldn't turn things around, but if we simply Wake Up our problems will vaporize, not instantly, but things will slowly turn around. So, it is essential that we Wake Up because that is the *only* way we can save humanity. I say humanity because it's only the humans that are in trouble. All the other life abides by the rule of nature, they live and die naturally. Humans may destroy some of that life along with us when we go, but the germs and bugs and animals, trees, plant life... all of it will rebound without humans around – it is only the humans that are the problem, and only because the humans think/believe that they are separate from the rest of nature, we think/believe that we are the caretakers of the planet, but we are only the destroyers, and only because we have misidentified with what we really are.

Many people, out of ignorance, are anxiously looking forward to this upheaval occurring because they think that Jesus in going to return and rescue them just before the upheaval, and then Jesus will send all unbelievers to hell. Such hubris is pathetic and is actually the result of jealousy, envy, and hate. *Mind vomit!* People always want to be the one who is 'right', and they want everyone else to be afraid that they just might be. Concomitant such thinking is that... ...by hoping and/or believing that something will happen you incidentally foster its manifestation. These folks just might get their wish, ...at least the first part, the upheaval end of it.

I do not subscribe to any particular religion or religious belief system, yet I do endorse all of the *mystical* messages entwined within religious writings. They all are road maps to the same underlying truth.

I will be quoting from the Bible and talking about some of the stories there. In my opinion, the Bible is the most misread, misinterpreted, and misconstrued spiritual book, yet also the most widely read book of spiritual guidance in the West, and therefore it is necessary to explain some of its analogy and allegory, and its contribution to the principle of

# The Dream of the Mind.

that which *'is.'* Unfortunately, the Bible is also the most
the versions of the spiritual message, precursor to countless wars, death, destruction, the killing of innocent people, and still very much in dispute, and argued about fervently, relentlessly, and endlessly. Being that it is one of the most published books of all time is testimony to the fact that within its pages lies a subtle message that all of us can intuit, and so immensely important that we are willing to kill each other to prove that our interpretation is right while the other person's interpretation is wrong, and it is specifically because of this egotistical determination to be the one who is right, the one who knows that their truth is right, and that yours is wrong, it is because of this stubborn vanity that we cling to the weak arguments and nuances in doctrine that keep us at odds with each other. The Bible has been used for power and profit rather than community. Rather than bringing people together the Bible has created division. I'm not saying that the Bible is wrong, only that it is interpreted incorrectly in almost every instance for political (power), monetary (power), and egotistical (power) reasons.

When I was a child I felt that I didn't fit into my place in the world – into the identity, and the story that I had been assigned. I felt very strongly that I was out of place – an observer rather than a participant. My parents took me to church every week; I disliked, and quickly grew weary of the stolid ambiance, the monotonous rituals, but I very much felt a presence that embodied me and everything around me – not so much in church as *everywhere*, especially when I was alone and my attention wasn't being absorbed by the activities of others – and particularly when I was outdoors, alone. There was a life-force, an underlying consciousness,

# Wake Up!

a single thing – *a singularity*  a *Oneness*, which we all share, which made our bodies and the physical world around us. The churches called this presence God, and gave this God much complexity and definition, but my intuition whispered to me that it was far simpler than that, yet intangible. I was too young to express it; I lacked needed experience, wisdom, and the etymological and semantic skills to explain the unexplainable, something that people have been unable to explain properly for millennia.

I grew up in the 60's and 70's in the upper Midwest. I fell into the hippie lifestyle (peace, pot, and microdot), and slowly became an inveterate drug user and an alcoholic. I simply could not accept or fit into the role that I was expected to assume in the great societal narrative that humanity has evolved into. So, I became a rebel, and things quickly went downhill for me. I quit school the day I turned 16, when I could quit without my parents permission. In the job market I was not finding success, and I was angry that not just the people I knew, but everyone who was finding success was – for the most part – doing so by fitting into roles, subscribing to the societal ethos, and being what society wanted them to be; and doing, for the most part, what society wanted them to do, and believing what society wanted them to believe, and agreeing to believe so – in most cases – without question, and oftentimes with patriotism and nationalistic fervor. You've probably heard the phrase: "Human doings, rather than human beings." I think it fits with what I'm saying except that I will change it slightly by moving the es's: Human**s** doing, rather than human**s** being. I refused to be a doer; there is a storm brewing concomitant this *role*-playing lifestyle, what folks believe, but most importantly, *how people identify with their personal narrative and individuality.*

I spiraled downward until... in the early 90's at the age of 35 things

# The Dream of the Mind.

came to a head, and something happened which entirely obliterated my conception of myself, and took from me every little possession that I had – quite literally – as though my home had burned to the ground with every possession inside. I fell into a state of dread. All hope was lost for recovery, and what happened did something that shook me so totally that I had a complete breakdown in *identity;* my identity vaporized, and I became nothing. It wasn't a nervous breakdown, not at all... ...not in a mental illness way, but it was certainly a breakdown in mental process – in mind process, and it tore from me the story of who I was. In a sense, I – sort-of – died, but I was still breathing, still alive; therefore, I had to continue along, but no longer able to function as the person (that character of the novel) I had previously believed myself to be. I recovered quickly, but my quick recovery doesn't diminish what happened. My identity vaporized, and I Woke Up to that which 'is.' Something I had known intuitively my whole life now became my very present, moment to moment reality. My name and everything about me became irrelevant, and could have changed now, although there is no reason to change what I now realized were merely labels, it was simply that my identity no longer mattered, and could easily be discarded and forgotten if I so chose. All the family pictures, records, birth certificate, etc., everything was gone, and my family ostracized me, thus making the loss of identity just a little easier since there was nothing holding me in that role. At this later date my family isn't really gone to me as much as I am gone to them – and in a sense I truly am gone, or at least that person that they despised is gone. That person no longer exists. They don't know that, and wouldn't accept it if I told them, and/or discussed it with them. I haven't seen them since 1985. I still had to live in this world though so I sent away for a new birth certificate and social security card (which, lol, are not easy to obtain when starting from scratch).

As a child I was particularly attuned to the subtle awareness. The younger we are the closer we are to the connection we have to the consciousness that underlies all things, and as we age we lose that connection quickly – particularly during the first few months after birth. As others around me became more and more separated from their connection to the subtle awareness, I remained closer, although I too was losing that connection – just not as quickly, but this tragedy that happened broke the surface of the pond – the ice, so to speak – and I fell through, into that awareness. Serendipity perhaps, but it could be that this was a result-oriented event – however tragic – to shock me into *Oneness*. I had been heading in the wrong direction, drinking and submersing myself in self-pity and resentment.

That which 'is' necessitates this book – I am simply a messenger. In other words... this book and message do not originate from me, but from that which is, the *Oneness*... and therefore it originates from *us*, not *me*, and the stories and allegories that I point to are evidence that this message comes from us, not me.

After many years of reading, observation, and contemplation about this, I now realize that awareness happens *very* rarely, and when it does happen, it is generally through traumatic situations or devastating periods of life. As people turn inward they sometimes use practices, but practices alone, although helpful, are unlikely to get you over the final leap because that last leap is very akin to actual physical death – death while still living. It's a very disorienting place to be – no one deliberately puts themselves there – and if they try they fall short. It is not a good feeling to have one's identity vaporize – at least, not at first. It can be very confusing when the

# The Dream of the Mind.

mind sees its own futility – *that who you are, and what you are, is not who you are, or what you are.* In fact... "who" is in itself part of the problem because you are not a "who" except relative to living in the physical world, and in reference to the human mind the "who" is simply – the individual – a narrative; a fictional story.

Also, without some exceptional traumatic episode or event there doesn't come a *need* to turn inward. A desire, perhaps, but a *need...* ...no. As long as a person is finding the things they need and want in the outward experience there is no reason to completely and irrevocably turn ones back on the outward and turn inward. Inward is boring and lonely at first, but if the trauma is severe enough that the person you are cannot continue to exist, the realization can occur that who and what you are is not really who and what you are; it is disorienting and depressing at first, and for some, it may be utterly terrifying; all of the sudden it seems that you are cut off from the herd – the human herd, the *identity* people; the dream that the humans live in is no longer your dream; it can be a feeling of irredeemability, and despair; plus, all of the glitter and attractiveness of the outer is no longer the true picture – you suddenly can see that the objective reality is rendered subjectively by most all humans in what I would best describe (using words) as *The Dream of the Mind.*

Humans are deeply invested into the dream of the mind – more than you can even begin to imagine.

But... it's possible to not only change to an inward journey, but also to see the outward for the specter it is – which requires a striping away, and not adding more. For this reason, this book cannot be long, the mind always wants more, and more just complicates things which makes matters worse. This is the same logic for creating simple allegory rather

17

than complex allegory – the mind wants complexity when in actuality, simple is better.

The only way one can step through the doorway to awareness in a single step would be to die. If, or should I say, *when* that happens you will be immediately back to what you really are, and that contentment will then wash over you, and this is why becoming aware while still in the dream of the mind is so difficult... ...you must effectively abandon your mind – jump ship. You must become – in a manner of speaking – *out of your mind*, and since you must also retain your mind to live in this world, this is essentially an impossibility, or at least a contradiction of what current human ideology and belief structures consider sanity. Some people, when they reach the bottom and there is nowhere left to go... they simply choose to die. Well... that's one way to Wake Up, but not my recommended way.

For a long time I thought that there was no reason to try to write this because no-one would take my word for anything – particularly what I am about to tell you about who you really are, or... better stated as: "what" you really are.

Now I realize that I am the one who *must* write this – only a person who is at the bottom is in the best position to lift everyone above him. Those people at the top aren't likely to bend and lift those below them, and those at the top are the least likely to become aware because they receive what they desire from the world, and have no interest in discarding that part of themselves that is so utterly captivating and provides them so much attention from others: *their identity* – a great part of which are their possessions. They are "in the world and of the world." I'm at the bottom already, no bending necessary. And then I realized, after putting this off... and off... and off... that I had to write it – the words were there, and I had

# The Dream of the Mind.

to get them out of me and onto paper, and I now know that I have a responsibility to write this; plus, I realize that I can't care if people don't listen. I do want people to Wake Up to the reality of what we are, but I'm not responsible if they don't. I can't invest my feelings. Very simply put – I have to write this, and put it out there for 'those who have ears.'

If you are one of those individuals who has ears to hear, then as you read this the words will become alive for you. You will know this is true simply because you already know this deep within you – but, until now, it has simply never been spelled out for you in quite this way. The further you get in this book the more you will feel it. You may not agree with every little thing I say, but that is the conundrum of words – we each have subtle differences and variations in our definitions.

Many people have written about transcendence, and many have done a fairly good job. I have read many books in my search for someone who could corroborate the information I am giving you, but have only found people who come close. In August 2020, while getting this book ready for publication I found this article on the web titled: "Could consciousness all come down to the way things vibrate."[2] Exciting stuff for me to see coming out! They are getting closer and closer, but not hitting the nail squarely. Many people understand that "you are not your mind," or they talk about "what is," or, that we are all one while keeping the "we," or they know that allegory is an important key to the puzzle... ...but it seems to me from what I've read that generally they couch their words carefully so to not offend – to appeal to a wider audience perhaps; or, they have part

---

2   https://theconversation.com/could-consciousness-all-come-down-to-the-way-things-vibrate-103070

of the information, but not all of it, so they are simply giving the best information that they can; or, often, they have some teaching or practice that they want you to use, or do – *an agenda,* usually with ongoing lessons or more information that will – supposedly – be helpful to you. And, in some cases, with a monetary requirement, or donations.

I don't care about offending anyone. Dogs bark! – that's their nature. And I'm not trying to gain a following. All I care about is spelling it out the best I can to help you to become aware – to "Wake Up."

That's all I care about! I don't feel a need to walk on eggshells, and I have no method or practice for you to follow. I will offer some tips such as don't watch TV, but no practices or soliciting. I'm not writing to give you something, I'm writing to strip away what you have. There will be no sequel to this book.

Something that I want to address early on here is that at any point in this writing – any comments I make that may imply a political or social tenet on my part, opinion, belief, or otherwise, is completely and thoroughly irrelevant to the message of the book. I am living in the world; to do so I MUST carve out an existence that is going to provide sustenance and to be socially involved. Therefore I have feelings, and those feelings will manifest in everything that I do – even in this book, but I am aware of this, so I will try to keep my subjective opinions to myself as best I can. Things that are happening in this world are irrelevant to my message, but with that said – I will talk about experiences we know about; shared experiences that I will use as examples to some of the concepts that I will be talking about.

I fully intend to explain to you the underlying nature of our reality

# The Dream of the Mind.

depicted in a literal manner never delineated with this accuracy, and also, I intend to explain what *exactly* is our mind, and how our identification with our thoughts and experience prevents our awareness of that underlying nature. For the reader this will involve a burning away of ideas and beliefs you have held true – I call it a burning away because it can be painful, confusing, and emotionally tumultuous.

This subject matter is 'tacit.' Wikipedia defines "Tacit" as: *"knowledge or implicit knowledge is the kind of knowledge that is difficult to transfer to another person by means of writing it down or verbalizing it."*

Implicit knowledge is knowledge that we know from within – such as intuition. I want you to learn here what people for millennia have been trying to convey... what is God? ...who is God, ...how is God? Hey... WHAT THE HECK IS UP WITH THIS INCREDIBLE UNIVERSE??? What's behind all this??? Well... ...explain to someone what a rose smells like. That's similar to what I'm going to do here for you.

Something else that must be addressed early is how some folks tend to conflate the word "mind – at least to some extent – with the word "ego." They must be distinguished.

The mind is our thoughts and the thinking faculty, whereas the ego is *identification* with a thought, memory, or experience as part of who you are – your identity.

We also conflate "mind" with consciousness. "Mind" provides *cognizance*; "Mind" allows our awareness of all that we see, touch, hear, feel, taste, smell, and our thoughts. Along with that our mind allows conceptualizing, and imagination, but "mind" is not consciousness.

## Wake Up!

Consciousness exists apart from mind and from here on out in this book if I refer to Consciousness – I intend it as *"Oneness."* I will explain in detail what the mind is later.

Words are *very* tricky things! Language, although a great tool, can also get you all mucked up, or even killed by simply uttering the wrong words. I will talk more about the limitations of words and language.

# The Dream of the Mind.

## The Nuts and Bolts

So...

When a baby is born it is the closest thing to pure consciousness that you will ever witness in a live human being. As soon as it emerges from the womb though, it begins to record things in its brain like a little data recorder, and that data recorder has a hard drive (brain) and a battery (a regenerative combination of organic cells with life span).

Even while in the womb, the fetus begins to experience things, and record things in its brain, but on a much more subtle level. When it emerges from the womb things *really* begin to whirl, and for the entire life of that person, all experience will be woven together into a story; a narrative that will become what we call 'ego.' And, that baby will grow and believe itself to be that narrative. The narrative will be that baby's (that person's) identity.

But, when the baby *first* emerges from the womb and you look into its eyes, you see a Consciousness that exists without a name, without concepts, ideas, purpose, not a single possession, not even a diaper, nothing there but Consciousness – and then, almost immediately, fear. For the first time, there is fear – separation fear. The baby doesn't understand fear but can sense its vulnerability, or its *nakedness* as denoted in the allegory of The Garden of Eden. The *Oneness* that inhabits all things has become an individual in the divine dance that we call life. The baby's *experience* will be its reality as it *learns,* through experience, to understand that which exists in physical form. First comes separation from the womb, then slowly from the Mother – that only thing that stands between the baby and death. The baby doesn't yet understand death or life, but at this early juncture, there exists an innate visceral knowledge that the mother is not separate, that the mother and baby are one.

Concomitant birth, a *seeming* separation from the *Oneness* has occurred, and the baby can – now that it is born into this world – only comprehend the world through its brain and senses, no longer aware of, and with no memory of the *Oneness* of all things, yet the baby can still sense its *Oneness* with its Mother and the bond between baby and Mother is boundless and unquestionable. Separation from its Mother – umbilically – only just happened. Up to this juncture (birth) the baby floated in amniotic fluid; all nourishment and even breathing were done by the Mother.

The underlying consciousness still exists within the baby – and always will; nothing changed for the *Oneness* we call divine consciousness – but now it is all filtered through the human body, and the mind, and all of the thoughts that the mind thinks are stored in the brain in the form of memories. The underlying consciousness that underlies all of what we call creation has become an individual and has metaphorically moved from the roots (below ground) of the Tree of Life to become a budding leaf (above ground), and at the moment of birth has bitten the fruit from the Tree of Knowledge and now must learn (obtain the necessary knowledge) to survive in this world. A grand narrative has begun that becomes our identity (ego), and we believe that we are the aggregate of all our experience which includes all the memories, and feelings that emanate from our experiences. We then tie all of our experience, memories, and feelings to our mind and designate it our *personal* soul. Much of our narrative is shared with others, and that becomes part of a *collective* narrative that is also part of the individual's

# The Dream of the Mind.

experience. But... *Oneness* hasn't actually become an individual... No... there is no individual... that is an illusion. *Oneness* simply inhabits – yet another – organism, and in this case – a human.

We all continue through life with a subtle intuition of our *Oneness* with the reality all around us, but we have been taught, we have learned, and we have accepted that we are separate. Our brain doesn't hold a memory of the underlying eternal awareness – *Oneness* – that we are all part of, but there is a subtle tacit impression that exists naturally within us of our *Oneness*. We breathe the air, we eat of the land, yet we have been taught that these things simply nourish our separateness, rather than our *Oneness* with the air, food, land, each other, and the world around us.

You were never born and you are never going to die. That is the truth. When read it may seem that I am saying that you never emerged from the womb (birth), and that you will never exhale your last breath (death). Oh... the birth into this physical world did happen, and a moment will come when you exhale your last breath in this body – but that's only relative to the physical; the underlying truth is that you have always existed and will continue to always exist, ...but, this is not part of your life experience. Your experience after birth is that you are separate, and that you are going to die, and you are going to die by yourself – alone.

This body you have, the world, and the universe you are currently experiencing, is only a momentary experience – only relatively real.

'Oneness': the *underlying consciousness* from which we all manifest exists on a subtle plane which underlies the physical universe and is intangible. Some people call this underlying consciousness the *Spirit World*, some call it *Divine Consciousness*, some call it *God*, some call it something else entirely. This underlying consciousness, which I will refer to as *"Oneness"* throughout this book, is singular, and we all share it. It is the source of all of the physical world and all that is tangible and intangible. Whereas it is possible to sense (intuit) our *Oneness*, it is impossible to see it or touch it until you first understand that seeing anything, or touching anything, *is* seeing all that '*is*' as a part of your self – *Oneness*.

Here is an analogy I have seen before.

With your mind you create thoughts, and like leaves falling from a tree onto a pond, those thoughts obscure the surface of the clear pure pond of consciousness that exists everywhere within you, and in all things. I have seen people call the underlying consciousness a 'pond.' This pond analogy is inaccurate and misleading, but it does have some good points. A pond is water, which can be clear and pure. A pond can also be pierced and entered – immersed into. As you get older, more and more leaves (thoughts) fall and cover the surface of this pond of pure consciousness. We can no longer see the pond, and to our mind, there is no pond, and we think that we are the thoughts and experiences we have stored in our brain instead, and we have no possible alternative but to agree – for how can you not agree with that which you believe yourself to be: your thoughts and experiences, and all of the ideas and notions that you have been taught by your peers, teachers, family, friends, who also are trapped by the dream of the mind; anything contrary would be insanity. You would be *"out of your mind"* – a very appropriate idiom.

The pond metaphor has that watery quality that one can be immersed into – which I like, but I think the "thoughts covering it like leaves on the pond" is misleading as to what *actually* happens that causes our delusion. Instead, let's eliminate the pond and look at it as a narrative, or book

# The Dream of the Mind.

analogy because it better illustrates the process that occurs, and – more importantly – the *story* that gets written, but it leaves out the pond.

When you are born the book begins; first page 1 obscures the underlying consciousness, then page 2. In the first month, the mind has written thousands of pages, and as you grow into your first year, hundreds of thousands of pages have been written. So, one's awareness of the underlying consciousness (*Oneness*) we share is hopelessly overshadowed as all precedence and interest is given to the pages of the narrative, and even the pages beneath the newer pages are becoming faded memories as the narrative grows. Then suddenly you are old, and there are millions of pages of narrative overshadowing the *Oneness* – and you can't even remember much of the narrative, yet the more the narrative grows the more the person becomes inexorably entrenched into it, but more importantly, and central to this book is that even if you could see what was under page 1 of this narrative, you have no memory of the *Oneness* in its non-human form, which is the reality underlying the narrative – though, not part of your life experience. Therefore, even if you could see under page 1 of the narrative, there is nothing there to see apart from that which 'is' – which you have simply misidentified.

It is your mind that you consider to be your soul, but you have decided – based on what you have compiled as your personal narrative – that you are the narrative rather than *Oneness*. Without your memories and experience you would walk around as *'that which is,'* but unable to function and survive in this world, ...but with the memories and experience you walk around as the personal narrative – able to function and survive in this world, but unfortunately, lost to *'that which is.'* Meanwhile, your body is aging, and the rate of cell decay is slowly overtaking the rate of cell generation[3] – and thus some dementia will occur, and ultimately... death – and you completely miss out on what you really are unless you can Wake Up before you die.

I want to describe it one more way that I think might help some people who don't like the analogies. It's not that the *Oneness* gets covered over by "leaves" or "pages." It is more like our thoughts are resonating (causing vibrations) so much, and we are so busy thinking that we can't stop the thoughts long enough to be aware of the very subtle connection we have with all that is. Either way you want to look at it... identifying with our thoughts and experience are the problem; identifying with those thoughts and experiences rather than identifying with that which 'is,' or in mystical term: the "I am" – that which exists everywhere and in all things.

Whereas these analogies may be helpful, all three of them fail to accurately describe what is actually happening. They are metaphorical allegories from which we might hopefully extract the truth from, but here in this book I will try to be more precise. These metaphors all speak to an awareness our thoughts obscure which implies that if we could stop our thoughts we could see this awareness plain as day.

Buddhist monks meditate for years trying to stop all thinking, or at least, to quiet their thinking to the point of awareness. They never can completely stop all thoughts because they are using their mind to stop their mind – a contradiction. They can focus on a mantra or a single sound/word/image, and whereas that may get them to a single pointed focus, that's simply a reduction – not a cessation, and it is only momentary because they will always have tangential thoughts. They sometimes speak of the silence between thoughts, but awareness of the silence between

---

3    In the brain cell generation is called "neurogenesis."

# The Dream of the Mind.

thoughts implies sensing that silence which again requires interaction. Even if they went into a trance and became completely single-focused on a mantra, word, or image, to the point of oblivion, they still need to be able to come out of the trance which makes apparent that their mind was ever-present and ready to intercede and bring them out of the trance. It is good to quiet your thoughts though. I wouldn't devalue the significance of quieting your thinking.

It is only in mind process that your narrative exists. Your memories and experiences are stored in cells in your brain. The mind is the field of energy connecting all the cells together that makes it SEEM like the narrative is a continuity – that it is a personality, a series of events and experience that has substance, and is in some way tangible, and real. Throughout this book I will admonish you to "not identify with your mind", but at the same time I mean: "don't identify with your narrative." The mind itself is not the culprit; the baby fresh from the womb has a mind, but no narrative. The culprit is the narrative and your mind simply compiles the narrative into a continuity. To identify with the narrative is "ego."

The metaphysics contained in these pages has been told over and over throughout history. Each time it is conveyed in a fashion suitable to the particular time-period, a particular culture, and the traditions within that culture. People need to be able to relate to it relative to what they see in their own lives, or it will be no more than nonsense, or it might be, or seem, anachronistic.

The Bible is a decent example of this anachronistic conundrum because it relies heavily on allegory, and it is very old, and its allegory is based on old truths that we know are not true anymore. Moses wrote many allegories and analogies in the first 5 books of the Old Testament, (if in-fact Moses wrote it, and/or was the sole writer), and when it became outdated, then Jesus brought new life to it through allegorical parables, and reiterated the same principles in different ways, and took it to a new level in a fashion that was relative to his particular time-period. In our time – the present time – we no longer relate to the allegory of the old or new testaments, so now people erroneously take those stories literally. The story of Jesus is actually the denouement to the allegory that was started in the Old Testament. If you look at the entire story it is sufficient in allegory – problem is... ...people take it literally.

The Bible starts out with how this vibration occurred, how the physical world, and then people, came into being. Then, in the Eden story, humans lose the connection with "God," or with what we call the underlying consciousness, and with what I call *"Oneness."* Then it continues along with the trials and tribulations of man's search for the reunion, and then in the New Testament Jesus brings it full circle into reunion, salvation, or reunification.

The Bible's mysticism is made more difficult because there are sections of the Bible that chronicle the history of the Jewish nation; stories which are historically literal – yet at times interwoven with mystical allegory, but the mystical message throughout the Bible is wholly allegorical. This is the very reason that Jesus always used parable (allegory), and analogies, in delivering his message – he wanted the people to *interpret* the allegory. By using allegory he did his best to make it difficult for people to misconstrue his teaching, and/or accuse him of heresy and kill him – which eventually he was unable to avoid. He wanted people to hear his parables and think about how they relate to their

# The Dream of the Mind.

individual experience – their own life, and thereby draw out the lesson relative to their individual life situation.   In many places Jesus used analogy rather than allegory, such as in his Sermon on the Mount.

Allegory should always be tailored accurately but with simplicity, and then interpreted loosely.   Loosely does not imply erroneously.   Every allegory can be understood in a slightly different manner for the individual – yet, with the same denouement.   For allegories of the transcendent type, the breadcrumb trail always leads to the same place.   When allegory is interpreted tightly the person ends up with a tortured interpretation that brings the allegory closer to the literal – and allegory is not literal.

But... now, in the 21st century, we have evolved to a point where we are better able to understand the concepts, science, and allegory of what is – so my message can now be more straightforward for you.   That's a good thing, yet besides the metaphysics (the nuts and bolts) of it, I want to also touch on several allegorical stories to show how the information has always been there; to show you that I'm not bringing you something new; and how those allegories are supposed to operate in your life.   I want to look at those allegories that are simpler... those which don't go overboard with minutia.   This needs to be kept on a level for all readers.   The truth is the same for any path, so there is no reason to over-complicate this.   If I use words that you don't know the meaning of – please be sure to *look them up!*


People believe themselves to be... the thing in the mirror which has a name, ideas, memories, and...   well, it's obvious that you are that person you see in the mirror that goes by your name, and has all of your memories, ...right?   And, ***relatively***, this is correct.

# Wake Up!

The truth about reality and what we call 'creation' is that it is a unified whole – it seems that there are different pieces, different objects, different people, different things, and *relatively* this is true, ...but they are all part of *Oneness*, just as the cells that make up your body are part of the entire being that you call your 'self.' Where there seem to be separate (individual) parts – it is relative to living in the physical realm. The mind gives us access to all of our experiences, observations, lessons from parents and teachers, and inculcation from television, books, social media, and other stimuli which are then stored in the brain. Our mind allows us to assemble all that is stored in the brain into a narrative – a story – a tale. Our brain is the repository for storing memories, and the "mind" is for accessing them simultaneously so we can think about them, but we are not required to identify with the mind – that's a choice, and when you learn to not identify with your mind – your choices in life – all of the choices you make – will become simpler.

I will be saying things that I may later seem to contradict. One analogy is sometimes imperfect whereas two or three might be better to help conceptualize a particular construct. Your mind may try to tell you that I am unable to make up my mind about the particular construct. Don't fall into that trap. What I am conveying in this book is quite tacit, and difficult to convey – much less grasp. As I write this I come up with new ways to say the same thing. This is important because we all conceptualize and see things a little differently. Also, words have nuances of meaning for different people, which we also have a word for: "*semantics.*" I will sometimes repeat something I've already said using different words, or a different arrangement of the words. I've already been doing this in the previous pages as you have probably noticed.

## Vibration and Resonance

"IF YOU WANT TO FIND THE SECRETS OF THE UNIVERSE, THINK IN TERMS OF ENERGY, FREQUENCY, AND VIBRATION" NICOLA TESLA

"The spirit moved upon the face of the water"[4] is a good metaphor for what transpired that brought the physical universe (creation) into existence. This movement upon the face of the water continues to happen each and every moment. It is a vibration. Movement upon water creates a ripple – a ripple is a vibration – and "the spirit (consciousness) moved upon the face (surface) of the water" is a great metaphor for the ripple created by the vibration, which is the movement that causes this moment – a continuous resonance; a vibrational dance. Back when this Bible verse was first written it was thought of as a movement on the face of water – back then they had no idea how frequency waves work. The only waves they knew were the waves on water – even back then people could see that throwing a stone into a pond made ripples or waves. These water waves were their best visual example. The Hindu's often call the movement, or vibration, a 'divine dance.' I have heard that the Vedic Scriptures of India also explain that vibration causes the material world to manifest from the spiritual realm. My knowledge of this did not come from reading Indian texts. I just came to realize how everything manifests from the *Oneness*, and its simplicity is *explicit* to me. It was later that I learned that Indian mysticism also embraces this same concept.

So... Your body (and everything that exists in physical form) has

---

4    Genesis 1:2

atoms and those atoms are made up of particles which "between observations... ... spread out like a wave over large regions of space."

A wave has frequency, (vibration, or resonance). What caused this vibration? The *underlying consciousness* which I will call *"Oneness"* caused it. Science believes there was a "big bang" which caused it – which is a fair postulate because a big bang would cause a vibrational after-effect.

A wave is a vibration, and the inverse is also true: a vibration is a wave, and it has frequency. The spirit moved upon the face of the water is a way of saying that consciousness, or I prefer to call it 'Oneness,' (most people call it God), has caused a ripple in the underlying consciousness (*Oneness*), or in itself. A vibration in *Oneness* causes a bubbling forth of physical reality out of itself – a bubbling forth of the most quantum particles.   So, what I'm saying is that the underlying consciousness (*Oneness*) caused the vibration, and the vibration is what causes particles to manifest in the physical world, and from particles come all of the objects: particles, atoms, molecules, cells that eventually make-up you, a rock, a tree, etc. This vibration continues to happen in each and every moment; if the vibration ceased, the physical world would disintegrate, vaporize, and vanish. The *Oneness* would be still – no vibration. By the way...   ...there is only one single moment – what is happening is happening 'now,' there is no other now, there is only this moment. I'll talk about the moment/now construct later in this work.

The physical reality – what we see, touch, feel, hear, smell, and for the most part, what we sense, bubbles forth from *Oneness* (pure consciousness). Just as a rock thrown into a still pond creates ripples that obscure our ability to see into the water – to see the bottom of the pond;

# The Dream of the Mind.

this is a reasonable analogy for how our thoughts create ripples which obscure or overshadow, our ability to be cognizant, or aware, of our *Oneness*.

It's a little more complicated than that though... What happens is that the ripples (thoughts) in our mind become memories stored in our brain, and we identify with these (thoughts/memories), and the resulting narrative that forms from all these memories, was created in a time-line (in sequence), and we then think we are the aggregate culmination of the narrative, and that we are separate and individual.

The ripples on the water can operate both as an analogy for how a vibration in *Oneness* manifests all that we call physical, and also can be representative of a subordinate, or secondary vibration such as *a thought,* which also creates a ripple on a more local level that interferes with our ability to be aware of the silent awareness that underlies the vibration that causes the physical universe. Just as everything in the physical universe manifests from the vibration in consciousness, so do our thoughts. Our thoughts are vibrations in consciousness. We can't be aware of *Oneness* because our thoughts are keeping our mind busy making it practically impossible to detect the pure silent calm watery *Oneness* that underlies our thought. *Oneness* is the basis of all things including our thoughts, and is omnipresent, and the source of all that is. Our thoughts resonating in our mind create ripples on our cognitive ability to see the calm silent pond, just as the leaves cover the pond, or the pages of the narrative cover the pond – all these analogies work to awaken us to what is preventing us from recognizing our *Oneness* that most people call God. Despite the fact that every religion I know of teaches that God is *'omnipresent':* present in all things, and present everywhere at all times, people always fail to correctly understand the correlation of God and *Oneness*. *"Omnipresence"* implies that it is all *Oneness*.

You might ask: But... if a calm stillness causes the underlying vibration, and we can't see the calm stillness because of the vibration that the calm stillness is causing, how then can one ever see or experience the calm stillness?

Well... You can't as long as you think of yourself as separate. You are the calm stillness, so a better way to think about this is: As the calm stillness can you see the vibration?

These concepts are particularly difficult to convey, and even harder to understand because we are limited by our inadequacies, one of which is language and words. I use the word consciousness to speak both of our cognitive state (you are conscious and thinking – consciousness) and the underlying awareness (pure consciousness, or *Oneness*) – which is confusing, and almost sounds contradictory. Therefore, I will *try* to stick with the word *'Oneness'* when referring to the underlying metaphysical – God/Awareness/Pure Consciousness.

I will try to use concepts and information that are more contemporaneous to our time.

Quantum Physicists now know that a particle can appear to us as a particle, or as a wave – either way. When an electron is observed it looks like a particle, but "between observations, the same electron spreads out like a wave over large regions of space. This alternation of identities is typical of all quantum entities..."[N. Herbert].[5]

At the most quantum level, it becomes apparent that matter is a wave

---

5   Quantum Reality: Beyond the New Physics, Paperback (2/20/1987), Nick Herbert.

# The Dream of the Mind.

(vibration) as well as a particle, or either – depending on observation.

Although the physics is incredibly complex and esoteric, the theory has been validated and is no longer just a theory; it is fact. This concept is beyond the scope of this book, but you can check into it by simply Googling it, or you can just check out "Wave-Particle Duality" in Wikipedia. The mind always wants more information, and less is better. I need to stick to that premise as I briefly talk about this and not go off point.

As a musician, I am aware of notes and chords, melody and harmony. I understand how notes can sound good together, and be harmonious, as well as how some notes can sound wretched together which is dissonance. Music can calm or agitate. We can cause people to feel better and relieve depression by using calming frequencies – which we can also do by simply putting out the right vibes...

All objects resonate; so do our actions and feelings. It is for this reason that we must learn how our actions and feelings cause harmony or dissonance. We need to study and understand this to the point that we can use it to make our relationships, our communication, our presence, and our community with one another be more harmonious, as well as to learn how to use harmony or dissonance to bring things to a close when we need to. Vibration, or Resonance, is a tool that we are very poor at using because we don't realize its immense importance; nor do we know – precisely – how it works.

Long ago, Buddhist monks accidentally discovered that when a small amount of sand was placed on a tight drum the sand would form geometric patterns on the drum as the monks chanted OM. The sand would form perfectly symmetrical geometric shapes as they chanted, and these forms would spontaneously change as they changed the frequencies of their humming, or as they added harmonies to the Ommmmmmm-ing they were doing. These structures in the sand are mathematical in form and become more complex as the frequency increases. Although the videos on YouTube that I am going to refer to are most commonly carried out on square metal plates these structures are not limited to the size or shape of these plates, and they manifest and materialize in circular formations – some of the demonstrations you can find on YouTube are done on circular surfaces, and the most revealing ones are done in water. Remember that the circle is an archetype, or symbol, of wholeness or *Oneness*.

There are numerous videos of people displaying this phenomenon[6]. It's important that you look at them.

This phenomenon is demonstrative of how vibration creates structure. In these YouTube examples sound is used to cause the metal plate to vibrate, and out of the vibration comes structure. Whereas vibration causes sound, in this demonstration we see how a vibration can be seen as both wave and particle. The vibration is a frequency of sound, and the metal plate is the computer screen displaying how structure is created by the vibration.

This is how the smallest of particles come into existence. The world bubbles forth from the underlying vibration. This phenomenon is simply a visual example of vibration producing structure.

Something that can be extrapolated by looking at this event on the metal plate, or even more so in water, is that what we are seeing is a small slice horizontally of what is actually a 3 dimensional event. If they can

---

6   Search for "sound frequency sand patterns" or "Cymatics" on YouTube.

# The Dream of the Mind.

create this event horizontally AND vertically, it will produce a ball shaped circular structure. This circular structure may not necessarily be exact in its symmetry, and may even have protrusions similar to how a virus looks, or other cells. Further, the progression of these patterns inevitably follow algorithmic sequence similar to Mandelbrot fractal geometry.

Just as you have seen a crystal glass shattered by frequency, all things respond to frequencies. All things: cells, molecules, atoms, particles, have their own frequencies and respond and react to harmonic frequencies acting upon them. This is called mechanical resonance. Being that all matter will resonate to certain vibrational frequencies we can therefore manipulate matter by using frequency and vibration. We simply don't understand how at this point, but scientists are always working on it.

All things bubble forth from the underlying consciousness (*Oneness*), and it is the vibration of *Oneness* that causes all of this. It is a single vibration that has a multitude of variation and subsets of frequency. All matter exists in its own subset or range of vibration, yet all are part and parcel to the whole vibration – *Oneness*.

Soon, we will learn how to use resonance to manipulate atoms and molecules. Then we will be able to destroy cells such as cancer cells simply by bombarding them with frequency, or we will be able to heal damaged cells by using frequency. All elements are subject to change through frequency manipulation. We just have to learn how to do it... if we don't destroy ourselves first.

The mind likes to think and imagine things. It likes to think so much that it never takes a break. And it thinks that it's usually right. All animals have cognitive ability (mind). Mind is a rather amorphous concept that I will explain later, but for now, I'll just say that your mind is

39

everywhere, and in all things, but where mind becomes 'you' it can access the brain to do basic thinking in order to solve simple problems necessary to survival, but humans have become particularly complicated due to a far more complex brain that provides for us a greater ability to formulate, conceptualize, and compartmentalize thoughts, ideas, and all of the objects into what we consider to be non-abstract constructs that we then incorporate into part of our identity, and not necessarily of the 'first person.' It can also be part of our identity as secondary to our person, such as that's 'my brother,' or that's 'my chair,' or that's 'my house,' or 'my money' – or even tertiary to our identity such as there is a planet about 2.5 billion miles away called Neptune that I can't see but I know is part of my reality, or there are fish that live deep in the ocean that people rarely see, and that I have never seen, except in pictures, yet those fish are a real part of my reality.

Even while we are sleeping the mind thinks, and we dream. But, when we are sleeping we are *subtly removed* from the physical conscious world, and therefore we lie closer to our *Oneness* than when we are awake, and *Oneness* can sneak past the mind's rationality sentry and speak to us using archetypal symbolism. Archetypal symbolism, metaphor, and allegory are the language of *Oneness*. Our dreams are surreal sometimes because of this.

*Oneness* cannot speak to us except through our memories, experience, and our imagination, (what we have in our brain). It comes to us in *imagery; i.e.,* pictures from memories of what we know from our physical world experience as well as collective experiences – Yes! We are able to dream the dreams of others (since we are all *Oneness*, it's not really the dreams of 'others'). We can also create dream imagery of people and things we have never seen as long as those things are consistent with our

# The Dream of the Mind.

experience(s) or imagination.

Thus, it is through analogy, allegory, metaphor, and parable that those who are aware impart to us this information of our *Oneness*. *Oneness* has access to all memories of all people and things, and *Oneness* can make those memories (images) available to all of us when our minds aren't ***on the alert*** to subject matter and ideas that offend our sense of identity. Our dreams are our own deliberate yet subconscious road map to awaken us, and the language of the dream is allegory, analogy, archetypal symbolism (motif), and metaphor. We are watching imagery in our dreams that is being scripted by our mind, or that was an image in someone else's mind that seeped through to us (which is rare, but happens more often than you would think); the *Oneness* is able to subtly influence our dreams when we are asleep. When sleeping our mind has less ability to obscure our *Oneness*. Our reasoning when asleep is thwarted, and with the reasoning faculty subdued, the minds ability to reason away what the mind considers unreasonable or unacceptable is weakened, and thus we are more amenable, and/or susceptible to the archetypal imagery, and allegory/metaphor, which can show us something we need to address in our life whether it be strength or weakness.

This was a fairly common practice in older cultures who saw their dreams as omens, or visions of portent. As we have advanced in knowledge and technology we have moved further and further away from being receptive to, or accepting of these motifs, and of trying to understand, and/or interpret their meaning. An excellent source for reading about the symbolism and meaning of our dreams is in the work of psychologist, Carl Jung. His book, "Man and his Symbols" was written specifically to address this issue for the lay-person. Perhaps an even more

41

important writer to symbolism and allegory is Joseph Campbell. Cultural Anthropologist, Joseph Campbell studied ancient cultures and found the same myths in different cultures to be so similar that they were telling the same story that had the same underlying meaning to these separate cultures. Campbell said, "The first function of mythology is showing everything as a metaphor to transcendence."[7] The words "story", or "myth" that Campbell speaks of is that which I refer to here as allegory. There is no difference. If you haven't read any of these two men's work – you should read from both of them should you wish to develop a better understanding of allegory, metaphor, analogy, archetype, and motif that is intrinsic to the bread crumb trail stories we write for ourselves. (If, that is... ...you find the information I am giving you insufficient.)[8] Although I have the highest opinion and reverence for both Campbell and Jung, they both fall short of bringing us fully to the transcendent state, but their work is an important bridge. Their work is also important to the broader import of what I am bringing to you in this book as not being new, that what I am saying is, and has been, available to us since the dawn of civilization. I think that Jung and Campbell could have been more overt about what they realized this all meant, but I sense from their books and listening to them on video that they were deliberately and very cautiously avoiding the quicksands of religious argument – which is where science meets superstition and speculation.


We are determined to become aware of our *Oneness* – even though we don't realize this. We are driven! We do it sometimes consciously, but

---

7   Joseph Campbell, The Hero's Journey: Joseph Campbell on His Life and Work.
8   There are also video's on YouTube if you prefer.

# The Dream of the Mind.

more often subconsciously. We make movies such as: The Wizard of Oz, The Lion King, Pinocchio, The Matrix, Avatar, Alice in Wonderland, Star Wars; we write books like Aesop's fables, Carl Jung's books, and Joseph Campbell's, ...or this book. We write songs about it like 'Turn, turn, turn,' by the Byrds, or 'The Walrus' by the Beatles: "I am he as you are he as you are me, and we are all together."[9] We create stories, movies, songs, little sayings, pictures, etc... You don't need to look far to find some image that is illustrative, or that symbolizes, or hints at some aspect of *Oneness*, or the transcendent archetype.

To a larger extent, we have religion and spirituality. Our highest institutions are churches. Myriad people go every week. We pray and make every effort to connect with God. HUMANS WANT CONNECTION! We are determined to become aware! – to Wake Up! Unfortunately the term 'God' has been sullied and is not practical anymore. The term 'God' implies something 'other.' It has too many false connotations, and myriad interpretations at this point, but that doesn't mean we can't mention it, we just have to use a different label for now. That's why I'm using '*Oneness*.' Is that the correct word? I don't know, I just need it for this book. The underlying awareness that we call God, or the spirit, or Yahweh, or whatever we call it is a single thing – a singularity; so it is *Oneness*, and it is everywhere, in all things, in this moment, now. Calling it "a" *Oneness*, or "the" *Oneness* might also be misleading because by preceding it with "a" or "the" has the connotation that *Oneness* is something "other." It's not "other" – that's only an illusion.

The underlying consciousness – *Oneness* – isn't interested in what we

---

9  Lennon, a mystic, contended these lyrics are jibberish... lol.... Wisely said!

43

own, possess, how much money we make, or have, how many children we have, how big our house is, how smart we are in comparison to others, how often we go to church, or even if we go to church at all. That which 'is': *Oneness* doesn't care one way or the other; it's our minds that have the duality; it's our minds that care, or not care; caring and not caring is duality. *Oneness* simply "is." The intent of *Oneness* is to simply 'be,' and to evolve into intelligent awareness while in physical form – and however unfortunate that we are having difficulty in this endeavor, this book is part of that process to 'Wake Up.'

When I look at you I now only see myself looking back. I realize that trying to understand this is aggravating because it can only be experienced – but, understanding to some degree what I'm saying will be part of getting to the experience. If you met me you would think that I am just another ordinary person – and you would be correct – it is only how I now see things and respond to things, that is different. People sometimes get aggravated with me when I challenge their constructs that they constantly use to describe and identify things. Not to be mean... just that occasionally an opportunity arises where I can show them how limited concepts and constructs can be. I have to use concepts and constructs too – I am stuck with the same language and words that everyone else is stuck with, but I try my best to negate people's constructs as much as possible because they need to understand first and foremost that the constructs are not ultimately real – only relatively real; mind stuff – useful in a relative sense, but constructs can be terribly destructive when held to be absolute truths, and incorporated into belief systems. I even negate my own mind stuff sometimes if I think that will help another person understand the movement toward awakening.

I can be talking to someone and think – just like you – that this person

# The Dream of the Mind.

is a real moron, but at the same time, I know that it is only my thoughts and beliefs, and their thoughts and beliefs, that are causing the concepts in their mind and mine, including the thought that they are a "real moron," or perhaps it might be their thoughts and resulting words or action(s) that caused my mind to think they were a moron. Beneath the mind and those thoughts is *Oneness* that we share, and that in actuality we are one in the same. It's the mind that is false. There is no moron – there is only the dream of the mind, the human mind which believes that the 'mind stuff ' is not relative, but objective and actual.

Many people might be curious about how I came to understand all of this, but all that is relevant is that you Wake Up. My story/narrative is not what we need to discuss or talk about, or that you need to wonder about. In fact, who I am in this world, and my story is just more minutia that would get in the way of waking up. More blah, blah, blah... My story would be another distraction, another obstacle; we need to eliminate obstacles – mind vomit.

While we are alive on the physical plane we need to survive, therefore we have evolved our brain. Human brains are more evolved than animal or insect brains, but all brains are evolved to effectuate survival. When we are born it is into a body, and in the body we can't remember the *Oneness* because the *Oneness* is not part of our memory because memory didn't start until *after* we had entered the physical and developed a brain; *no place to store a memory without a brain,* and therefore, there is no memory of anything before we had a brain. Can't remember something that we have no memory of! We can only remember back to the point of having a brain – a place to store our experiences, our memories. Our

45

*sense* that there is more to this existence is where intuition comes into play.

At birth we become an individual – or we *think* we are an individual, and relatively we are, and while in this body we experience the world through our senses, yet there is also a very subtle intuition that we also possess which is shared by all of us – an intuition that is stronger in some and weaker in others. Despite our *relative* individuality and autonomy, *Oneness* is intent on getting us to Wake Up to what we *really* are while in this body – to get us to make the connection to *Oneness*.

It sounds like I'm saying that something 'other' than ourself is trying to do something to us (make the connection to *Oneness*). This is not a contradiction because we are *Oneness*, and that's all we are... ...so, another way of saying that *Oneness* seems intent to get us to awaken to our *Oneness* is to say that we are trying to get ourself to awaken, or... "I" am trying to get this. We are all trying to "Wake Up" to this! It is soooo easy for us to trip up in this concept. The entire message is that there is only *Oneness*. I'm not making a grammatical error when I use the word "ourself." When I use "ourselves" I am creating duality again; In fact, simply using the word "ourself", and the word "I", while not grammatically incorrect, using these words does imply a duality for the person trying to grasp this. ....but, all I have is our language to convey this concept to you – I'm stuck with words. You have to grasp it – be patient.

Words and language are very powerful, but also extremely limiting, and often – powerfully limiting, and in most cases – to some extent – misleading. You have to be able to get past this limitation. I believe that you can. I am stuck with language and words, a semantic quandary, so

# The Dream of the Mind.

you need to keep in mind as you read this not to get stuck by some grammatical error on my part, nor semantic gymnastics. I am not above making grammatical errors. I'm also trying to explain this in English. English is particularly difficult, but English is my language, so... I have to do my best, and my best is the best I can do. People have been trying to explain this for thousands of years, and it's still as mystical as it's ever been. Humans have a love affair with words, ...just look at poetry. We love the art of word-play. Consider synonyms... words that mean the same thing... often with very subtle differences... and then, it also depends on the person who might have a slightly different understanding of a particular word than you or I.

Look at the word *Oneness* which I use as a synonym to the archaic word "God." Some people would use other words to talk about God or *Oneness*. Underlying Consciousness... or the Self... or The Divine... or Lord... or Creator... The list can be lengthy. Although words are necessary for communication, and can be useful, words can also be monsters at times, and can be obstacles to understanding one another.


A vibration in *Oneness* is what makes the various objects, "and the spirit moved upon the face of the water" is good imagery for helping us to understand that the spirit (God, or *Oneness*) moved upon the surface of the water (again God or *Oneness*). Where many people will get stuck in thinking that the 'spirit' is one thing and the 'water,' another thing. This is not the case. They are both the same thing – it's a metaphor – a picture, so to speak, of an action. Water is the superlative earthly metaphor for consciousness. You might ask why a metaphor would symbolize a force acting upon itself. The answer to this I keep repeating: There is only one thing – a unified whole – in and of itself. What else can it act upon if there's only one thing? That's the conundrum. *One becomes Many, yet the Many are but One.* Through the act of acting upon itself, or creating a vibration of itself, all of this incredible magic happens – a divine dance – that we see as all these different things – that we think of as "other" than us. *Oneness* doesn't make a vibration that is separate from *Oneness.* There is no 'other.' *Oneness* is what vibrates. A simple vibration... ...look around you – AMAZING! ...isn't it!!!

Even the air in front of you... look at an object in front of you... even the air from your nose to that object is made up of atoms and particles... there are atoms extending from the tip of your nose to that object... it seems like there is space but there is none... it's an illusion caused by the density of the objects... air has very little density... the air moves easily when pushed. Air is real and an equal part of this crazy incredible system.


*Duality* is the nature of things that exist on the physical plane. There is White and Black which happen to correspond with Light and Dark. In between are all the other colors. This fact, that there is a spectrum between White and Black is illustrative of the fact that it is simply one complete thing. It's similar to the front of something and the back of that something. In between is the rest of that one thing. It's just one thing – White and Black are simply the two ends of that one thing we perceive as an entire spectrum of color. We have hot/cold – and varying levels of hot and cold, good/evil – and varying degrees of good and evil, male/female – and a spectrum of sexuality between very male and very female, and that list goes on and on, but I'm not trying to fill pages with opposites. All I want to point out about the opposites is how even they are indicative of

# The Dream of the Mind.

one being many, yet many being one.  Someone might argue that there are many different spectrum's of light each caused by a different frequency or vibration... and that's true, but all of the spectrum's combined make white light.  Black – *defined in human terms* – is simply a lack of color. *Oneness* is the whole vibration which encompasses ALL of the physical universe, and within *Oneness* there are myriad sub-vibrations or ranges of vibration.  And when I say "myriad" I mean countless – all can be divided more.  All of the quantum particles have frequency or a range of frequency.  A frequency is a wave and a wave is a vibration.  These particles are sometimes attracted to one another.  They become atoms and then molecules and then cells, and organisms, or inorganic matter such as rocks.  Organisms that are similar are closer to each other in frequency. Humans have their range and as such are attuned to that particular range more-so than other animals, but all animals are within a range that is somewhat similar.  Animals are in a range; trees and plants, rocks and minerals, but **all** are inherently some underlying vibration – *Oneness*, or what some people call God.    These things often are not a single frequency; usually they comprise more than one, or many frequencies. Some of these frequencies are basic to all things, e.g., humans have minerals in their blood, so we share those frequencies with minerals.  All particles have a frequency and those particles join to become more complex particles, atoms, molecules, cells, and as they do their frequencies become harmonic.  Sometimes these harmonies can be dissident.  This is where stress can cause problems – the harmony is disrupted and a dissonant change can result.  With organic life this might manifest as an evolutionary change, or more often – what we call disease, and disease eventually results in evolutionary change.

# Wake Up!

Things that manifest in the physical world have duality: sort of like a front and a back; all things have frequency – same is true of sound and light. Then, there is what is in-between. It can't become part of the physical world without having a front and a back, or beginning and end. One extreme to another extreme; from one end to the other end; from one side to the other. This is duality.

The whole vibration encompasses all the sub-vibrations, and all the sub-vibrations are embodied within the whole. The One becomes many, yet the many are but One.


In the beginning was the Word, and the Word was with God, and the Word was God...[10] Words are vibration. *In the beginning was the vibration, and the vibration was with Oneness, and the vibration was Oneness.* This again is a wonderful analogy and metaphor, and synonymous with "the spirit moved upon the face of the water." In Hinduism, Brahma, who represents the creator, first shows himself as the golden embryo of sound. He was a sound, vibrating outward, and the sound echoed back upon itself and became water and wind (a nice metaphor). OM is a term that has been labeled by some as the sound of the primordial vibration. These paths are all mystic messengers for us – paths that we have created our self to lead us home to our true essence – our underlying reality. In Greek philosophy and theology, we see the word "Logos" which means "word," "reason," or "plan," the divine reason implicit in the cosmos, ordering it, and giving it form and meaning.[11] These paths, stories, allegories, will forever haunt us as long as we don't

---

10 John 1:1
11 Definition of Logos from Britannica.com

# The Dream of the Mind.

embrace the truth about our *Oneness*.

I have heard Christian scholars equate 'Word' in this verse with 'Jesus': "In the beginning was Jesus, and Jesus was with God, and Jesus was God." I have heard this many times in Christian circles, but this application is incorrect. ...but then, Jesus was an embodiment of vibration just as you or I, so maybe it fits if you want to look at it that way – but then, you could just inject your name into the verse.

Pluck a string on a guitar, cello, violin, or any string instrument and that string will vibrate in a pattern of a figure 8, and it will make a sound that corresponds with the frequency of that vibration. A sound thinking that it is an independent sound and not the vibration is similar to our mind thinking we are an individual rather than a symphony of vibration ...of frequency. Is it not ironic, or perhaps premonitory that our symbol for Infinity is a figure 8 lying on its side.

"You will look for me, but will not find me, and where *I am* you cannot come."[12] I like this very mystical saying. This is in reference to you while in the physical body, while you believe that you are your mind – while the narrative is still real to you, and you believe that you are the story that started when you were born. Where I am you cannot come, means that as long as you identify with the mind you will fail to know that which 'is.' The "I am" is the Oneness. The individual believes himself/herself to be separate from all the "other" things. So..., where "I am" (the many are but one), you cannot come because you believe

---

12 John 7:34

yourself to be 'other,' or where (the one has become many).


Ego is the word that psychologists have given your identity. They call your connection to the person in the mirror: your identity, "ego." Psychology is *pseudo*science. Science considers psychology to be pseudoscience, not just me. Psychology isn't true science at all – it's a bunch of hunches and guesswork – often good hunches and guesswork – which is where science begins, but true science moves hunches and guesswork into the empirical and quantitative.

Psychology cannot do that. In essence, psychology tries to study the *narrative* of the mind and find commonalities and patterns that will help the psychologist to understand how people become neurotic, delusional, or demented, or in some way out of touch with what other human beings see as normal, or what humanity has *decided* is normal. Sort of like going to the library and reading all the books by a particular author, and then trying to analyze patterns in the narratives to understand what makes a certain character tick; a fictional character that doesn't even exist; or perhaps to understand the writers by their writing style, and what they wrote. Psychology may be considered a "soft" science. It essentially studies the narrative that I speak of in a book which we call our identity. But, the narrative that we build throughout our lives isn't real, it's only relative, and could be revised, or completely rewritten at any time. All are lost in the narrative until awakening takes place, but it is the psychologist who is the most lost. I consider Psychologists to be *Priests of the Mind.*

That doesn't mean there isn't value in psychology such as the work of Carl Jung who studied the subconscious dreams and archetypal symbolism found in our dreams – but Jung's work had an anthropological schema that

## The Dream of the Mind.

set him apart from other psychologists – and anthropology *is* science.

Funny thing though... is that it is *within the narrative* where psychology resides, and the only place it resides. Psychology is the study of our personal narrative, as well as the collective narrative on each level... and if the narrative is only relatively real... ...well...

Something I commonly see is that most of those who write about what they call: The Underlying Consciousness (which I call *Oneness*) tend to get stuck in focusing on our difficulty dealing with emotions and psychological problems, the pain we experience, and how it gets in the way of our becoming aware of our *Oneness*. I don't want to say that all psychological problems are nonsense – sometimes the brain can have actual physical damage to it that causes psychosis, or there may be a chemical imbalance. But what I can say quite confidently is that the more common emotional and psychological neuroses that we usually encounter are no more than mind vomit. Learn to not identify with the mind, and mental problems cannot exist. Who and what you believe yourself to be is a compilation – a narrative, ...or narrative's' because in some cases people have more than one narrative that they have going on in their mind. If there is something wrong in the mind on a personal level, on an individual level, it is information in the personal narrative, and identifying with that information, that is causing the problem, and it has nothing to do with the brain. It will affect your feelings, but if you understand that it is your identification with your thoughts, memories, experience which is causing the feelings, then you are on the road to assuaging those feelings by not identifying with them. Instead of helping the individual with understanding the mind to be a narrative/a ghost/a spectre/an illusion, the psychologist will instead use drugs to attempt to subdue the mind and resulting feelings, to numb it down, to dumb it down – to render it harmless, emotionally dead, paralyzed, anesthetized. On the other hand, if there is something wrong with the brain such as a brain disease, or a chemical imbalance, ...that is a physical malady, and has nothing to do with the information in the narrative, although if the physical malady, or chemical imbalance, is effecting the neurotransmission, then the mind could suffer an inability to reason properly – but still, this is a physical problem that has nothing to do with the narrative. Identity with the narrative – a story that is only relative – is what we label: "Psychology" (mind vomit). Diseases and malformations of the brain or chemical imbalances in the brain are "Psychiatry" which is quite different from psychology. Many people are so entrenched into identifying with the narrative that they will not be able to escape it... or, not without a traumatic event to shake them loose.

How can you possibly find the "I am" when you fail to see that you are it – when you believe that you are a separate entity altogether – perhaps better characterized: "a separate 'identity' altogether." It's like trying to find your belt when you're wearing it.

Of course, you do have to go to the bathroom by yourself, and eat what's on your plate, and pay your rent. You are an individual to that extent. But... 'individuality' is *relative* to existence on the physical plane. The individual is synonymous with 'identity,' and 'ego.' You are not actually separate or apart from the essence of 'what is' and it is in and as the 'what is' (*Oneness*) that we all exist. That which 'is' does not exist as the individual – that which 'is' exists as all that is – which includes the individual, but is not limited to the individual. The physical arises from the vibration; the vibration does not arise from the physical, although ...while in physical form we can cause secondary or subordinate vibrations

# The Dream of the Mind.

– especially through our thoughts and feelings, which are simply an extension of the original vibration. By simply moving you are causing vibrations, which causes a change. Use a tool – you cause a vibration which causes a change. Move something – you cause a vibration which causes a change. Even a simple thought causes a corresponding vibration which causes change. Essentially, we are able to slice out sections of the original vibration – which, when we do it, we think that we are changing something that is 'other.' But... it is never 'other': we can never create a separate vibration that isn't part of *Oneness* – or part and parcel of the original vibration. The changes we effect are more like extracting water from hydrogen or separating a distinct shade of color from the entire spectrum of color. We can cause a change, but it's only relative to the whole - "*Oneness.*"


When humans think of awareness and of things that have awareness they think of things that move. Humans associate movement with conscious awareness. Well... not quite; we don't think that a cloud is conscious just because the wind is moving it along, or that a car is conscious just because the motor is moving it due to the energy created from burning gasoline; but when we see movement that moves of its own accord, and especially of its own volition, we tend to associate that with some sort of consciousness. The more movement something has, the more awareness we give it credit for having. Now I'm going to tell you something that may seem a little unsettling, or difficult to accept: *Even the chair you are sitting on has awareness* – you just don't see it moving, but it's moving much more than you are aware of. It doesn't have higher cognition, or what we recognize as brain function, but it does have awareness that is not apparent to you. The chair isn't aware that it's a chair, but at the atomic and particle level throughout the chair there is awareness. All things have awareness at the atomic and subatomic levels. We associate conscious awareness with movement... well, if you could shrink yourself small enough you'd see it in action.

Just as there are colors that you cannot see. So... the cloud does have awareness, but not because it's moving from the wind – it has awareness because it is made up of atoms, and those atoms are moving purposefully and methodically, the cloud as a whole may be getting manipulated by the wind because the cloud has low density, but the atoms are doing their best to stay close to all the other water molecules, and every particle that makes up the molecules that have become the cloud are caused by a vibration that has frequency and awareness. It's just very hard for the human mind to comprehend this subtle form of awareness – but it's very real. But then... you can't see certain colors either, or hear certain sounds that are outside of the human range of perception, so... it's not too surprising.

When I look around the room I see many different objects, and I know that I am that, and I am that, and I am that. And, I know this explicitly – not as a theory or postulate. I know this explicitly! It is only your mind that thinks of you as separate. Your body does not think it's separate – it is only your mind that thinks. Your body is just a gazillion atoms with electrons racing around in huge orbits that you can't see. Those atoms in the table or chair don't see themselves as separate from you. They are simply aware that they *are* – not that they are a chair or a table – they just are. Lucky for them they don't have a brain and a mind because the brain and mind cause us as much trouble as delight. Just look at human beings, the dilemmas and drama we create for ourselves – what a mess! Sometimes atoms lose an electron, or gain one; this is due to a corresponding vibrational change, and this will cause a molecule to become a different substance altogether – and we see that as 'change.'

I spoke of how we have evolved our brain because on the physical plane we have to survive. It's important to note that all of the bugs, animals, plant life and all organic life that exists on the physical plane have evolved to survive. A gnat has no less part to play in this elegant dance than you or I. Even a cell, molecule, atom, or particle have an equal part to play. We are all part of a whole – don't let this fact slip your awareness. The wolves need the deer. The deer need the grass. The mosquito's kill off those animals that become vulnerable to the mosquito. And believe it or not, the deer need the wolves too. There are viruses, germs, parasites, and predators that all have their purpose. Rocks have minerals and trace amounts of those minerals are in the food we eat and in our bodies. The Earth is a very elegant and fragile ecosystem that needs ALL of its various parts if it is to support this particular fragile ecosystem of organic life. It's a grand symphony that we call life. From one comes many, and the many are but one.

*Oneness*, through the process of evolution sometimes produces things that end up being unnecessary, or become useless. These things die off, or they may vanish through attrition. Actually, they don't go anywhere... ...they simply *change*.

"Let those with ears hear." "Let those with eyes see." These lines reveal the tacit nature of *Oneness*. Awareness is not for the faint of heart, nor the fool – just as Dorothy found out in The Wizard of Oz. What is written in these pages is the single most important thing for humans to understand. Out of all the books I've read that talk about this topic, this one will be short as possible, and straight to the point. At times it may seem that I am meandering around and getting off track, but I am writing extemporaneously, and then editing, and my only intent is to keep *you* on track. I don't expect every paragraph to be unflawed to your thinking. What I hope for is that your thinking is open and open to perspective – everyone has a colloquial way of saying things, and I need the reader to understand that. I'll do the best I can with the words, but as I said... words are tricky.

The mind always wants more information. When in agreement with a topic, system, or belief, the mind craves more information because the mind craves the euphoria of *knowing,* – or of at least believing – that it is right – the mind craves affirmation; and if the mind disagrees it will then crave more information because it wants to find an angle of attack, some fodder for argument; to find, or at least conceive of, a flaw in the opposing logic. Since the mind is simply the aggregate of our experience, intuition, beliefs, etc., the mind is dependent on itself, or other minds, to ratify and/or verify information – information that is almost always open to interpretation. For instance, if you don't know the meaning of the word aggregate in the last sentence, your mind will tell you that you can derive the meaning of aggregate by its context to the rest of the sentence, and then if you agree with what is being said in the sentence the word aggregate will mean something that helps you to agree, but if you disagree with the rest of the sentence then a word or a perception can help you to disagree. This can happen very subtly, and often subconsciously. Always look words up if you are in any way unclear of their meaning.

We have science in which information is verified through empirical

# The Dream of the Mind.

systems that are logical, rational, and use good common sense, but these systems are once again a product of the mind, i.e., human beings developed them, and they can be argued, and argument requires an opposing viewpoint, which gives way to interpretation, and thus stalemate. Our systems use instruments and machines to help us measure, record, and analyze the data we collect, but once collected and measured it is turned back over to the mind – yours or someone else's – for interpretation, for definition, for meaning. The mind wants to verify things, and to do so uses systems that are always a product of the mind – someone's mind, even if not yours. This is why humans can agree on very little. This is why this book is short, and this is why we have throughout the ages used allegory as our breadcrumb trail leading us back to the truth of who and what we really are.

When using the mind things cannot be explicitly resolved. This is due to language barriers, belief systems, perception, and opinion. Everyone has a right to their 'opinion.' The Earth was once the center of our universe; that was an opinion, and it was heresy to oppose that 'fact' on the pain of death.


So, before we go any further, let me explain what the mind is. This is of paramount importance to understand.

## The Mind – the Illustrious Tyrant!

To understand any of this properly, we need to understand exactly what our mind is, because without this understanding – we're trapped.

People may say something like: "I've made up my mind;" or "I have this idea in my mind," but what is your mind?  Doctors and scientists can't point to it.  Where is it in your body?  Some people think that your mind is synonymous with your soul.  Some people believe that your mind is your brain *in process*.

Wikipedia puts it this way:

"The **mind** is the set of thinking faculties including cognitive aspects such as consciousness, imagination, perception, thinking, judgement, language and memory, as well as noncognitive aspects such as emotion. Under the scientific physicalist interpretation, the mind is housed at least in part in the brain. The primary competitors to the physicalist interpretations of the mind are idealism, substance dualism, and types of property dualism, and by some lights eliminative materialism and anomalous monism. [3] There is a lengthy tradition in philosophy, religion, psychology, and cognitive science about what constitutes a mind and what are its distinguishing properties."[13]

Well... Wiki just makes it more confusing.  It's elusive, and can't seem to be nailed down.   But... it's not that hard – it just can't be proven

---

13 Cut and Paste Quote from Wikipedia.

# The Dream of the Mind.

empirically – at least, not yet.

Most everyone including doctors and scientists believes that thinking is done in the brain. This is inaccurate – not wrong, but not accurate. The brain and mind work in conjunction with one another, but it is the mind that allows us to think – to form ideas, concepts, form sentences, etc. But, what is the mind exactly?

To be precise... The "mind" is the *electrical field* that permeates the billions of neurons and cells in the brain and throughout the body. The brain, on the other hand, is simply a storage device that only holds and/or stores information – somewhat similar to the hard drive in a computer. The mind doesn't *hold* the thoughts and memories in your brain – the mind only provides the electricity to store things and set little electrical switches and provides the conduit to access all of those cells instantaneously and keep them all charged properly.

The mind is an electrical field that facilitates instantaneous connection and communication between all the cells in your brain and your entire body which provides the *sensation* of cognition that we call "mind." Therefore, the electrical field is – in essence – what we call 'mind.' It is the instantaneous connection of all the cells which hold our memories and experience that facilitates our cognizance – so *it seems* like there is a "mind" – and it is the electricity that provides this. Your mind is an electrical field.

This electrical field exists throughout the body and brain through your cells and nerves which act as an electrical *grid* not unlike a wiring harness, except that there are no wires. A reasonable analogy would be comparing the electrical grid that connects the billions of neurons in your brain to the wiring harness that connects all of the electrical components of your car together. Without the wiring harness (grid) and the electricity (electrical field) your tail lights won't work, your spark plugs won't work, your headlights won't work, your instrument panel won't work... ...nothing will work – your car will be dead. There is a circuit board in your car that turns a light on in the dash if the oil temperature gets too high, or the tire pressure too low, or if your seat belt isn't fastened, or many other events that might happen in the car, and it all seems to happen instantaneously because electricity is so incredibly fast. And none of this can happen without the wiring harness connecting it all together – so, there is an electrical field (electricity), and an electrical grid (the connectors).

In your brain, there are no wires. Instead, the wires in your brain, and your entire body, are replaced by neurons and neurotransmitters (chemicals) which allow the electricity to flow throughout your brain and nerves. I may sound repetitive, and many readers probably already understand that you have electricity and connections in your body, but I want to make sure that all readers have the best chance to understand this as I go on – so bear with me.

Even with the wiring harness, your car is still dead without the electrical field (electricity), and the same is true for your body: even with the neurons and neurotransmitters, your body will be dead without the electricity.[14] So, what I'm getting at is that the electricity is to your car what your mind (electricity) is to your body and brain. It is the electricity that allows you to think – your mind is an illusion that is caused by the *electrical field* that flows through an *electrical grid* of neurons and neurotransmitters – and where the nerves seem to stop, the cells take over

---

14 Of course, I'm not missing the necessity for the cells in your body – including the brain – need for $H_2O$ and Oxygen. Water is an electrical conductor, but we know that, and it's not necessary to include every bit of detail to explain this.

and this connecting continues – I'm not going to be able to be exact on the physiology, or the chemistry – but it happens right down to the quantum level.

When the electrical field (mind), and electrical grid (neurons and neurotransmitters) are up and functioning normally we are alive and conscious – and thus, we conflate 'mind' with 'consciousness.' When the electrical field goes down we are dead – plain and simple.

However, if the electrical field (mind) is up and functioning, but the electrical grid is damaged (*as in the case of brain damage),* then we are mentally handicapped to whatever degree, or if there is extensive damage to the brain, we may lay in a hospital bed completely brain dead on life support, but the body doesn't rot as long as the electrical field is active. With damage to the brain, the connections (electrical grid) in the brain may be damaged, but that doesn't affect the electrical field (mind). Depending on the extent of damage to the brain, minimal signals may still be able to be sent that keep certain organs working; sporadic limited dreaming may occur, but depending on the amount of damage to the grid (the nerves and neurons), ...without *fully functioning connectors* thoughts and – particularly – *cognitive thinking* is either limited – to whatever severity, or non-existent. ...I can hear you knocking, but you can't come in! ...hehe!

With age we have a slightly different version of the same thing happening; the brain can atrophy and we can develop dementia which is the slow version of ending up in the hospital bed brain dead. Eventually, dementia – or Alzheimer's disease will atrophy the areas of the brain which regulate our heart pumping, and central nerve system working, and that person will die. With a younger person who suffers brain damage, (who's brain we know is not atrophied), we purposefully keep their body alive using machines in the hope of reviving them.

The mind (electrical field) could be likened to a staging area which we use to assemble, disseminate, organize, and process thoughts – temporarily. Most of our brain, on the other hand, simply stores information like the Hard Drive of a computer. There are areas in the brain that regulate vision, hearing, keeping the heart pumping, lungs working, and the other senses, but these areas are more akin to regulators, and/or controllers. What I want to talk about here is thought processing – how you become '*you*.' It is the thought processing and storing of these thoughts that build the narrative of who we think that we are – *our identity*.

The brain stores all of our memories and experience, and the electrical grid (nerves and neurons) connect all of the cells together where memories are stored, and the electrical field makes it fluid so that we can see those thoughts/memories simultaneously – all together, like a collage of pictures. With the help of the electrical field (mind) we are able to – fluidly – arrange and rearrange these pictures (thoughts/memories) however we want to form ideas, concepts, beliefs, or to further develop and expand existing ideas, concepts, beliefs. We may think that there are areas in the brain that are cognitive, but this is slightly skewed. It is the electricity that allows cognition function. The reason people think cognition happens in the brain is due to the fact that the electrical synapses facilitate the recollection, arrangement, and rearrangement of all the memories and experience we have stored in the brain, and it all happens so lightning fast that we have the sensation of what we call "mind."

# The Dream of the Mind.

Scientists believe it is in the frontal areas of the brain where most of the thought processing occurs, and I wouldn't dispute that for I am not an expert on brain physiology. What I will attest to is that nobody has been able to identify where the mind is in your body. And what I am saying is that there is no mind... ...and that what we call the mind is simply the instantaneous connections of all stored memory and experience – and we can call that "mind" if we want. Your mind is an illusion brought about by the electrical *field!* It is the electricity that makes the connections in your brain concurrent – the electricity makes thinking possible. So... yeah, your mind is – in essence – the electrical field.

Another way to say this is: The electrical field – which we call "mind" – is essentially the ability to access myriad memories (information stored in the brain) simultaneously, or what seems instantaneously, ...made possible because of the speed of electricity, and a bit of chemistry. Different people have different ability on this stage depending on brain function, chemical balance, and luck. But... for the purposes of this book it is enough to know that what we call "mind" is your ability to seemingly float and process disparate memory, current observations, feelings, intuition, experience, and other stimuli *simultaneously* for thinking purposes. Another little picture of how to think of it is to think of it sort of like having a mobile where you hang all these memories and stimuli from, where they can float about in front of you, and you can look at them, rearrange them, look at them from different angles, analyze them. That's what the electrical field does for you. Saying that "mind" is synonymous with "electricity" is not inaccurate because – as I have said – your mind is quite literally an electrical field that flows throughout all the cells in your brain making connections *seem* instantaneous, which gives us our autonomy. Because the 'electrical grid' actually uses 'electricity,' and since the distance between areas in the brain are relatively small and electricity incredibly fast, the brain can bring myriad memories into cognition so incredibly fast that it seems simultaneous, this is how humans become "*me*." The speed of electricity makes it *seem* that all of our thinking is happening simultaneously in one central location – and relatively thinking, our body is one central location, as is our brain on a more local level.

It sounds like I'm saying that ALL of our memories stored in our brain are available to us all at once... and they are, but we can only recall those memories relative to the experience we are currently experiencing, and/or the memories that are relative to current thought processes. Some people have better ability on this stage than others. If ALL of the information in our brain was made cognitive all at the same time there would be an information overload – therefore we have filters and switches.

With a newborn baby, the electrical field (mind) is flowing, and the brain is highly functional, but there are no memories, no experience, so the baby is a blank slate, and must acquire memories and experience in order to establish an identity. Since a baby has few memories to review, the baby is more of an observer and data recorder with no extensible analytic ability. As we age memories and experience accrue in our brain, and our ability to analyze and formulate ideas increases and we make judgments, form ideas, develop concepts, belief systems, have insight – which becomes our *personal* narrative – the individual.

The instantaneous connections in our brain are vital for conceptualizing new experiences, and for assembling the memories stored in your brain into cognitive thoughts which you need for survival, to function socially, and to be creative. They aren't actually instantaneous,

# The Dream of the Mind.

but they are so bloody fast that you can't notice or sense any latency. As you think those thoughts and resulting changes are then stored into the brain while new thoughts take shape in the electrical field (mind). As long as the *electrical grid* (neurons and neurotransmitters) is intact, and the *electrical field* flowing, this goes on and on, and the brain is continuously filled with these thought memories.

Your mind and brain working together record all experience, and all of the changes that you sense, and these changes are then stored in your brain in what seems like a linear movement, or *time*-line. At any moment these memories can be accessed and brought into cognitive awareness in the mind, but they sometimes fade and can be forgotten. The entire brain is involved in this process, but I need to keep this as simple as possible. It is the concept of *what the mind is* that I'm trying to impart to you – not the science of how the brain works. When the brain is healthy and the electrical field is working properly and the electrical grid (neurons and cells) intact, working properly, and not damaged, we walk and talk and share our narrative with others; if the memories and experiences stored in the brain cannot be accessed due to some injury, degradation, or atrophy of the brain, then we are considered retarded, or worse – we may lay in a hospital bed on life support and we are considered brain dead; if the electrical field (mind) quits functioning altogether, then we are just dead. The electrical grid might be just fine, but if the electricity isn't flowing through the grid, we are DEAD. If the electricity is flowing, but the grid is bad for some reason, we can still be alive, but not functioning well. So, while the brain is necessary to store the memories and experience of our narrative, it is the electrical field that allows us to be cognizant.

In what I have explained we find that *the mind is a process... the process of retrieving memories and experience from all areas of the brain, body, and senses into an instantaneous and spontaneous amalgamation of sensory and experiential reflections.*

But, the entire point is that it is the electrical field (mind) that allows cognition/awareness; the brain on the other hand only stores the information, and the electrical grid (neurons and neurotransmitters) is the highway that connects all the different areas and cells in the brain. But... with that said, you are much more than a mind. The rabbit hole goes deeper. Mind, like everything is an aspect of *Oneness* – limited by your memories and experience. Humans identify with the memories and experience and believe themselves to be that narrative – that story. This is why ascetics try arduously to quiet their mind... ...to sense their *Oneness*. But, *Oneness* is never the individual. The One becomes Many, yet the Many are but One.

So... as I continue along here, whenever I use the word "mind" I am referring to a process that occurs that results due to an electrical field that exists throughout your body that allows you to access instantaneously all thoughts, memories, and experience that are agent for your cognizance – and that which humans call "mind."

Unfortunately, we identify with the mind as who and what we are, and we do so with such intensity that we even imagine that the mind is eternal – so we identify this electrical field also as a soul.

We have the word "ego" to label our identification with the mind. But, the two must be differentiated. The ego is identification with the narrative, the story of our life that is the result of our thoughts, memories, and resultant feelings – which derive from our experience.

The mind, on the other hand, is the electrical field that facilitates

# The Dream of the Mind.

access to these thoughts and memories; ...but – in our head – "ego" and "mind" are conflated into the same thing, but only because we identify with them both – roughly – as who we are.

Ya know... humans make up these words – like 'ego' and 'mind' and we are stuck with them to communicate. I don't necessarily like or dislike these words – they represent concepts, and concepts are just concepts, but I have to use them... I have to have some anchor, a common thread in order to explain this.

So, what allegory does – quite elegantly – is it provides a tool to overcome the adversity and acrimony of contradicting opinion. We have found a road-map to the truth that cannot be nailed down. The Wizard of Oz is an excellent road-map, but it can be misinterpreted by those who oppose its transcendent meaning in any way they choose. Jesus' use of parable in this manner was – at the same time – deliberately both incisive *and* divisive. So, with allegory the *interpretation* can be argued without changing the allegory, two opposing viewpoints can coexist, and thus the allegory (road-map) remains unsullied. People will argue my interpretation of the Wizard of Oz, but – remarkably – they won't change the story-line – it will always remain intact, leaving the breadcrumb trail intact, which is the beauty of allegory.

Allegory, Metaphor, Analogy, Parable, and Archetypal Imagery are the language of *Oneness*. I've talked about how we are determined to become aware, and that we have consciously and more often unconsciously created stories to lead us to the truth of our true nature, our being. Let's get into some of them and look at how they work.

The story of the Garden of Eden I have never heard interpreted correctly – it may have been explained correctly at some time in some place, but I, myself, have never heard it explained the way I'm about to, which is strange because this allegory is rich with imagery and archetypal symbolism that very elegantly outlines the mystical message of the 'fall from grace' – or, better said for modern times: *being born into the physical world.* The fall from grace is simply our losing the cognitive connection, or our awareness of *Oneness* – or 'God.' A "graceful state" is that of contentment, and contentment is a sort-of balance between calm and agitated. A sort-of 'equanimity' that I think is best described using the word 'contentment.' The fall from grace is the transition from a graceful contentment of the subtle underlying consciousness, to the agitated state (the mind) concomitant life in the physical world.

I have recognized the fiction of the mind as have a few others, but when born we lose that connection, and it's *very* hard to regain it. People get PhDs (D.Th.) in Theology just to learn about God, yet they don't have a clue. They have simply studied the dreams of the minds of those who came before them. Awareness does not come about through matriculation... ...and actually, matriculation is more likely to solidify and entrench the mind into identity with the narrative, which expands upon and solidifies the Dream of the Mind, making it simply more fascinating. On the other hand, thoughtful introspection and meditation (turning inward) can help puncture the veil and provide a glimpse of that which 'is.' People who study religion are studying the idea that we are 'other' – that we are separate from "God"; individuals with individual souls which is not correct. Something fascinating (at least to me) is that all of the theological schools operate under the spell of the minds obsession with remaining in control **within** the Dream of the Mind, and then existing after death for eternity as that individual; the narrative of the individual, the dream of the mind. An inescapable circular trap! The mind is our greatest enemy and our necessary ally. Keep your friends close and your enemies closer.

There is a peaceful contentment that you become immersed in when the truth washes over you, and you see for yourself the beauty and elegance of *Oneness*. So, here is the meaning behind the allegory of the garden of Eden. It's pretty simple really.

## The Garden of Eden

This is a great allegory.   Beautiful imagery, rich in motif, and archetypal symbolism.

So...  There is this garden.  And this garden is in the East.  East is the archetypal motif of where things begin – the rising sun – birth.  And, what happens in gardens...   ...things grow, things are born, they take root. Gardens provide the nutrients for the beginnings of things we grow – making it a superlative metaphor for the beginning of things.

So...  in this garden, there is this "Tree of Life."  Even the name implies allegorical context and archetype.  A tree as we all know has roots into the ground – in this case, a rich loamy garden soil.   The ground is a good metaphor for the border between that which gives life – the fertile biomass under the ground where it is dark and where dead things decay and feed those things like the tree, providing what it needs to live, and above this border – the above ground where the tree blooms; where light abounds, and life is abundant.   Below ground is metaphorically consciousness in its pure form (*Oneness*), and above ground is metaphorically the physical world we experience.   Humans associate Below Ground with death and decay – being six feet under; Above Ground with Life and Light.

This is a family tree.  Just like we talk about when we say: "Our Family Tree."  The trunk of the tree is a good image for the life-force to move between the roots and the branches.  Today we use the image of the tree to represent our family – the tree is a very good metaphor for this purpose.  And the tree is always growing and dying – winter to summer – things come, things go; in winter (the West - evening) the leaves die, and

# The Dream of the Mind.

in the spring (the East - morning) new ones come. Each branch represents an ancestry, and the myriad branches and shoots represent new communities, families, and the leaves may be seen to represent – in this allegory – those who are living at this time.

Consciousness transitions from the non-physical realm (below ground) to the physical realm (above ground) via the roots of the tree. Ostensibly, the Eden story Tree of Life seems intrinsic to humanity alone, but the metaphor can be taken to mean all life, but regardless, *all* that is in the physical world is represented by those parts of that tree that are above ground.

Then, over yonder in another part of the same garden we find the Tree of Knowledge, once again, a tree with all of the implications including the roots below ground that represent the underlying consciousness, which is important to remember since all that exists, all that is, even knowledge, comes from this singular place – this underlying consciousness (*Oneness*). One notable difference is that this tree bears fruit, a metaphor for both reproduction and nourishment. Things must die for us to live, and here at the tree of knowledge we become inextricably married to the Earth, the dance of life and death. The Tree of Knowledge depicts our need for knowledge and nourishment to survive in the physical world, and the *decision* to take nourishment, and become a part of the life and death cycle. Biting the apple is a ritual representing a signing-up – an agreement to participate in the Life and Death cycle. All of the myriad branches and leaves in this tree represent all of the fields of knowledge, all of the ideologies, all of the biased opinions and belief systems, all of the scientific knowledge, all of the places you can go in your mind, and the mind can go so many places that a tree is once again a good motif for this metaphor. The leaves can also represent each of us in our particular place in this analogy. The fruit of this tree indicates not only the nourishment we need to sustain us, but also that one form of life gets consumed (dies) to sustain another form of life. A life and death cycle. Our communion with death.

Now that you are living on the physical plane you need knowledge to survive, which requires a brain to store the knowledge you gain through experience in the form of memories, and then you need a mind to access these memories to make associations. Memories are necessary for survival in the physical world. You must remember that when you touch fire you get burned and that the wolves that ate your friend would be happy to eat you too... so run! Adam and Eve were told that if they ate from the Tree of Knowledge that they would be subject to death... ...and so... ...eating the fruit (taking nourishment from the physical world) from the tree of knowledge is a metaphor for entering into a symbiotic relationship with the physical world, and to do that you need the knowledge to survive, ...and having been born into the physical world you are now subject to the rules of the physical world which includes death and decay.

You must take nourishment from the physical world, (eat of the apple), become part of the cycle of life and death (things must die for you to live), and later... you must also die and your body becomes nourishment for other new life, (accept your mortality – which are the terms of this contract from birth to death).

When you are born you must acquire knowledge to survive (physical life requires memories, thought, senses... a mind), and you now have a body that is part of that which is physical – but importantly, any memory

# The Dream of the Mind.

of the *Oneness* was **not** carried over and entered into your brain... ...so now it appears to you that you are separate, or at least you believe yourself to be separate – which is analogous to having free will (individuality) in the sense that now you have to make individual decisions, and act autonomously. You have bitten the apple (taken birth, acquired free will – to make your own decisions, – and you've no memory of the underlying consciousness (*Oneness*)). Now you have to make individual decisions in order to survive in the physical world.

The Tree of Life is a representation of life bubbling forth from the underlying consciousness, and the Tree of Knowledge, which also bubbles forth from the underlying consciousness, implicates your nakedness (vulnerability) to the elements of the physical world, and your need for knowledge (mind) to survive, as well as your marriage to the life and death struggle.

Upon biting the apple, Eve recognized her nakedness and covered herself – she protected her physical vulnerabilities. The nakedness spoken of in these verses from Genesis does not connote 'shame' as we are taught to believe but instead, it means naked *vulnerability* – our vulnerability, and ultimately – our death. There is no shame in the human body – never was. Shame of the human body is mind vomit.

Funny thing that when you Wake Up from the dream of the mind you reawaken to the fact that you were never born, and you will never die. Yes, the physical body will wear out and die, but you then know that you are not separate from the *Oneness*, that you *never were* separate from *Oneness*. But, when we are born we don't bring our former awareness of *Oneness* with us, and until we Wake Up death stands before us like a great chasm that we can't see into – a scary place.

# Wake Up!

A common animal found in dreams is the snake which is also known as a serpent. Snakes, which can be quite deadly, are typically feared by humans making them a perfect archetype for fear, death, and transformation. This snake represents those elements of the dark side or shadow element. Snakes shed their skin which is metaphorically a transformation of rebirth – becoming new and leaving behind the old.

The snake or serpent of the Eden story is representative of the transformation from being *Oneness* into the illusion of being apart from *Oneness*, i.e., birth. The metaphorical one (Serpent) who sheds the old for the new guides the plebes (Adam and Eve) into the physical world. The snake in this allegory is wrapped around the Tree of Knowledge – not the Tree of Life.

The snake's action of enticing them to eat from the Tree of Knowledge serves to allegorically deliver the woman and man into the delusion of being separate and individual – of being born into, and vulnerable to the physical world – of being naked; the transformation from the *Oneness* to being the narrative (your memories and experience). The woman eats of the fruit that causes the earthly appearance of separateness.

Fruit is fruition. The fruit here not only represents our need to consume life to maintain our own, but also the apple is the fruit of the tree, just as Eve will bear children as well, and all must – ultimately – become food for the next generation. The eating of the apple is ritualistic, an initiation, like baptism, of our new role, and with it... earthly knowledge – being human – having a mind that cannot remember *Oneness* with that which 'is' – due to a physical body and brain that doesn't retain any memory of the movement from *Oneness* to being human!

Killing is a shadow side action in the human psyche, and we must kill

# The Dream of the Mind.

and consume what we kill.  The snake is a killer, venomous, slithery, on its belly – the quintessential motif for shadowy dark-side behavior.  The whole story is incredibly rich in motif, allegory, and archetype.

Of course, we don't really shed our *Oneness*; the allegory is instructive – not literal.  We retain *Oneness* while at the same time not remembering it.

The allegory is meant to awaken and instruct us to what happened – how we became separated from *Oneness* (but we never really are separated from *Oneness* – because we are *Oneness*).  This story is current and relevant to each new person who is born.  I'm somewhat mystified that this story isn't told in this allegorical context.  I have seen this story explained in an allegorical fashion, but not the same.[15]

As humanity has evolved so has its allegories.  With our understanding of evolution and genetics we are able to write stories that follow the actual path of the evolution of mankind, and all of the life we find on our planet.

It's one thing for a human to have a breakthrough to the understanding that a connection was lost with what we really are, and it's another thing altogether to be able to see into the past and watch organisms evolve from a primordial soup, and eventually become what we are today.

So, what I'm getting at is that the *breakthrough* – which is very very very difficult can be made less difficult when aided by some evidence and images to help see the delusions of the mind – how the mind tricks and

---

15  You can Google: Allegory and Garden of Eden.  I would list a couple of websites, but websites come and go – by the time you read this, things will have changed.

traps us.

Modern conveniences such as the printing press, and now electronic storage devices have made it much easier for us not only to research but to record our discoveries, our ideas, our thoughts. Moses wasn't able to connect the dots for evolution – Moses knew nothing about evolution.

Adam did come from the dust of the Earth, as we all do, and Eve was of the same flesh (which comes from the same source). All life comes from the dust of the Earth, and just as surely – returns to it. On the bigger scale, the dust of the Earth comes from the dust of stars.

The Eden allegory is anachronistic to our time. The fall from grace and loss of our connection with 'God' is a constant truth, conceptually intact throughout time, but the evolutionary part is knowledge-based, and has changed as our knowledge has grown.

There is considerable dialogue that happens in the story of the Garden of Eden, but the imagery is more significant than dialogue, or locution. The imagery is still quite valid, but the dialogue is anachronistic – or it is my opinion that the dialogue is not helpful anymore. This story was told in a manner contemporaneous to its time-period, for people living during that time-period, in the perceived understanding of people who were primitive by our modern standards.

The Bible is loaded with stories that are allegories, and verses that are analogies and metaphors. Sometimes they are easy to identify because they have some magical element like someone being turned into a pillar of salt, or all the animals the world over somehow congregating into a ship. The story of the great flood has been told in several different versions. It was told in "The Epic Of Gilgamesh," and the Welsh Flood epic: Dwyfan and Dwyfach, and in Noah's Ark, inter alia.[16] These deluge stories are all

# The Dream of the Mind.

allegories of rebirth; a cleansing by washing away and starting over – rebirth. The story of Sodom and Gomorrah is a story of walking away from an unawakened state, or a hedonistic – morally decrepit – lifestyle, and changing one's focus to inward, instead of outward, *without looking back*.

Critics may say I make too easy an allegory from these stories, but they are not that hard – once you know what they are and how they work. The Biblical allegories often mix into the allegory characters who actually lived. This can make the allegory confusing. The story and death of Jesus is the culmination of what started in the Genesis story of the Garden of Eden. How Jesus' life is *described* is where it becomes allegorical. I'll get to that.

Today, these same messages are being told in allegories relative to our time. Allegorical symbology is prolific in our books, plays, and movies, but my favorite, and where I think the transcendent allegory is told most elegantly, colorfully, and simple fashion is in The Wizard of Oz.

The greatest magic is the magic of *Oneness* which has – very elegantly – used a process we call evolution to resolve problems in diversity and weakness. The magical *quality* of *Oneness* is the most elegant of magic but isn't magic at all in the *hocus-pocus* sense.

The allegories tell us who we really are, what we really are, that we are one, and that we are that which is eternal, and exists everywhere all at once; this is far more magnificent and magical than any story of angels or continuing on as a being that is stuck in the prison of being an individual soul.

---

16 Search Google for Versions of the Great Flood.

# Wake Up!

The magical quality of *Oneness* doesn't need the hocus-pocus that our minds have invented as magic: *Abra-ka-dab-ra, a rabbit out of nowhere* – which is nonsense – fake magic – mind vomit! The vibration of consciousness is a far more elegant and miraculous magic than anything we can conjure up (hocus-pocus style) in our minds – you have to think about this – about how this symphony of life – the divine dance – has an incredibly magical quality. There is no other kind of magic.

We invent magic tricks that are only tricks because we want to see the magic happen right before our eyes – but true magic does happen right before our eyes – it's just that we cannot replicate it to manipulate things.

We can only see true magic as a quality, not as an action! We can see a baby being born and see the magic in that action, yet it's not the Abrakadabra type of magic – it is a magic of quality, the quality of the action of birth. Love can have a magical quality; walking in the woods, or looking out upon some majestic setting can have a magical quality. The recognition of this incredible beauty causes a magic in the heart. An awakening that is magical in itself.

The brain is governed by the laws of physics just as much as the atom and the universe; micro to macro – macro to micro (the one becomes many, yet the many are but one). Just because the brain has evolved in a manner to retain memories, and the mind to make connections in the brain to extrapolate data and enable abstract thinking, makes it no higher than a birds brain and birds mind which does the same thing for the bird and keeps the bird alive.

The human mind likes to think, and it tries and tries to convince us that we are superior, but the more we think, the more garbage we have blocking our connection to consciousness, and it is this garbage heap

# The Dream of the Mind.

which is in actuality the barrier to awareness. Our superior intelligence is a double-edged sword. At least the bird is more attuned to its place in this physical world, its very fragile existence, and its inextricable connection to its surroundings.

In the end, your body feeds the maggots and bacteria just like anything else. All is one. We are not superior – we are the same. The mind will need to dispute what is written here, and for some people what is written here will be what they label as heresy, and they will study what is written here more than anyone, but only to try to refute what I'm saying – such is the conundrum of the mind.

It is when we interpret the mystical as literal that we want the continuity, that which is eternal, to apply to us as an individual. We want to have an individual soul. The ego (identity with the narrative) won't give up! It has to be real – it thinks so, and boy... does it like to think so!!! – it is determined to prove itself!!!

The ego is a false sense of what we are, and it needs the fake story – the narrative – to be real in order for the ego to continue along after death because the ego is no more than a narrative. The ego needs to believe that we will continue along as a soul after we die when in actuality, the soul is only the mind. There is Bob Smith when he is alive, and then there is Bob Smith's soul (a narrative) after it supposedly leaves his body behind upon death. The identity with the life narrative of Bob Smith has convinced Bob Smith that he is an individual soul and that he can rest assured that he will exist forever as the same individual soul even when the body is dead.

You are much more than a silly little $=<100$ year story/narrative. That is the dream of the mind. The ego will never accept its demise even though there is nothing it can do to change the fact that when the body dies, the electricity in the central nervous system stops, and therefore the electrical grid in the brain – which is also connected by tiny nerves and neurons decay – cease to exist, and therefore connections in the brain are no longer made, memories die as the brain cells die, the mind ends, and the narrative ends – end of story!

Of course, there remains electricity in the dead body, but now it is localized to the atoms as they spin and move about. Change is still occurring, but local to the molecules, cells, and atoms in the body. There is no longer an electrical grid working in the same fashion as it did while you were experiencing cognitive consciousness.

This concept of the individual soul is simply backward. When the body dies an individual soul does not disembark from the body. There is no 'individual' soul – never was. Nothing leaves the body. The *Oneness* always simply 'is.' The *Oneness* inhabits everything, including all matter, and all the bodies everywhere. All the bodies exist within the *Oneness*; the *Oneness* doesn't exist in little pieces – each person getting his or her little slice of the pie. When a body gets old and can no longer regenerate cells, and it is worn out, it simply dies... nothing happens to *Oneness* that inhabits *everything* – including that now dead body. That's right! *Oneness* still inhabits that 'dead' body, all of the cells, all of the molecules that make up those cells, all of the atoms that make up the molecules, all of the particles that make up the atoms, and even beyond that... ...but the brain function has ended, and the mind no longer exists, the mind which simply facilitated the creation of a narrative of an individual experience. The one becomes many, yet the many are but one.

# The Dream of the Mind.

The lights in your house can illustrate this. The bulbs are like our bodies, and the electricity is what makes them glow. When a bulb wears out the electricity that lit the bulb doesn't go anywhere – the electricity stays the same. The electricity in this illustration can be compared to *Oneness*. The electricity that lights all of the lights in the whole house is the same electricity. It's not like there are more than one electricity, or that there is a different electricity for each bulb as though each bulb gets its little slice of the electricity pie. The bulbs simply wear out – the electricity that would normally make the bulb glow simply can't make the bulb glow anymore because the electricity can't pass through the filament because the bulb has failed for some reason, most likely the filament in the bulb is burnt. The bulb is worn out; the bulb is dead – it's not the fault of the electricity. You are not your body – to think so is a misidentification, a misconception. You are the *Oneness* that inhabits EVERYTHING.

Another analogy could be a balloon filled with air. When the balloon is popped the air doesn't go anywhere – it's still right there. It wasn't that the air left the balloon, it's simply that the balloon wore out or suffered catastrophic failure, and could no longer function; the air simply merged back into the air that the air always was in the first place. The balloon itself, like the light-bulb, will simply rot, decay, break down into its constituent elements/atoms/molecules and re-form into something else – the cycle just continues; nothing even misses a beat.

It's important to remember that what I have just explained are only analogies; the electricity and air are made up of properties in the physical world – atoms/molecules/electrons/etc., – and that which 'is': *Oneness*, is not *merely* the physical world, and is not limited to physical properties, but for the fact that *Oneness* does inhabit all that exists on the physical plane, and is the source of the vibration from which all the physical universe arises.

Same as my analogy for electricity, and for air, is true of *Oneness*. It doesn't go anywhere; it's simply that your body is worn out and no longer functions. It's the ego (your mind) that wants us to believe that the body contained an *individual* consciousness and that there is more than one electricity (the light bulb), or more than one air (the balloon), or more than one consciousness (an individual soul). You don't go anywhere because you never went anywhere; you don't lose anything because you were never more than that which 'is': **you are not your body** – or as Dorothy learned: "If I ever go searching for my heart's desire, I won't look any further than my own back yard, because if it isn't there, then I never lost it to begin with." Your ego (the narrative) wants you to believe that your mind is your consciousness. Your mind facilitates cognizance, but consciousness (*Oneness*) exists despite the personal narrative. Such hubris is the nature of the ego from which your individual identity arises.

Some people may think: "what's the use then – life is futile. I will be gone, and that's it." The mind wants desperately to survive and it will try to trick you (the mind is tricky), but this mind thing is so ridiculous. Bob Smith and the story of Bob Smith doesn't need to continue along because Bob Smith didn't exist to begin with – it's a narrative – as I have said. You need it for living on the physical plane – it's useful in that way. When you die; (oops, there is the conundrum again: you never die), but, when your body quits working, what happens is that everything returns to normal. Don't think that it's futile. It's life on the physical plane that causes the illusion. You may think that if you (the false self – the narrative) can't go

# The Dream of the Mind.

on then it's all futile, but when your body quits it will be an 'aha' moment – there will be no despair or confusion; everything will be crystal clear as never before since before *you* – *the narrative* – came into existence. No worries folks! When your body wears out – which it eventually will, and the body dies, it will be similar to waking up in the morning. When you wake up in the morning it's like: Oh yeah... never-mind – I was just dreaming. Same thing when your body dies. You will wake up and immediately realize – oh... never-mind, that was a dream – the dream of the mind. So, dying is more like waking up than it is going to sleep.

***Except that*** – even what I have just said isn't entirely accurate, (words and language are deceptive), but I have to be able to give you examples and analogies. Language is incredibly limiting.

*Oneness* won't wake up when your body dies – ***it's already awake***. It won't be surprised either. So... it won't *actually* be like waking up because what you *really* are is already awake – it's only your awareness of it that is obscured by your narrative – *a failure to identify properly*. If you are living the dream of the mind, then death will be a bump, but if you Wake Up to your *Oneness* of that which 'is,' it will be a seamless transition. That's what this book is about... Wake-Up! You can Wake Up now, and the dream of the mind ends, or you can continue along and suffer. Start right now to consider yourself a part of all that is, and the illusion of separateness will slowly begin to fade. Soon it will not be "consider," it will be a realization that all you see 'is.' Always the seer and never the seen. The Buddhists say that all life is suffering. While you live in the dream of the mind this is true. When you Wake Up to the dream of the mind it is still true, except that ...things get much easier as you become more and more aware that what is happening in your mind is a fiction that you needn't have much investment in.

Our heart's desire that Dorothy is speaking of in the Oz story is our re-connection with consciousness – to Wake-Up. We have this inkling (intuition) of what we *really* are: the *Oneness*, and we are driven by that inkling. Dorothy learned that she had never lost what she was seeking and that it was within her the whole time – not outside of her. The Wizard of Oz is a story of 'Transcendence.' There are many stories of transcendence that exist today. Many were written purposefully and consciously, and some have been written by people who the message was channeled through, but who were not fully aware of the importance of the story they were writing – but even those who were unconscious of the transcendent aspect of what they were writing knew that they were trying to speak to that principle of higher power. They had an 'inkling,' a hunch, a foggy impression.

Jungian analyst Marie Louise Von Franz in her study of fairy tales (which are allegories) pointed out: *"I have come to the conclusion that all fairy tales endeavour to describe one and the same psychic fact, but a fact so complex and far-reaching and so difficult for us to realize in all its different aspects that hundreds of tales and thousands of repetitions with a musician's variation are needed until this unknown fact is delivered into consciousness; and even then the theme is not exhausted...."(Emphasis added)*[17] In this quote we can see again my simple phrase: *The One has become Many, yet the Many are but One.* Thousands of variations to understand one simple psychic fact.

The incredible transcending ability of consciousness (*Oneness*) to bring us this message – in many cases through disparate parts written by

---

17 The Interpretation of Fairy Tales, [24]:1–2 (chapter1). Marie Louise Von Franz.

# The Dream of the Mind.

people who were not themselves aware, is in itself indicative of 'what is,' the 'I am.' One aspect of its magical quality is its transcending ability to get through to us – regardless of our "fall from grace." We have all of these different allegories or versions of the same allegory with different characters and theme, but alluding to, and resonating with the same light at the end of the tunnel. Always the seer and never the seen! When you look about yourself continually be aware that: I am that, and that, and that... This awareness will help to break the illusion.


Yes, The Wizard of Oz... ...and it's directed at children – a child audience. That's brilliant! That's why most adults miss it – they think it's a story for kids. I am inclined to believe that Frank Baum wrote it this way purposely because people need to start learning this at an early age, and adults weren't listening because as we age we become more rigid in our ego – more bound to our identity.

Same with "The Lion King" but I like the Wizard of Oz. Our minds become more and more certain that we are who we think we are, and that what we think must be so. Baum was onto this, perhaps. What does the Bible say? Something to the effect that unless you become as children again...[18] "Unless you become like babes..." ...as I have pointed out: looking into a newborn's eyes is the closest you can come to seeing the underlying consciousness up close and personal. I love this story.

The real beauty of The Wizard of Oz is its simplicity. It's intended to be a story for children which underlies the importance of starting this

---

18 I don't like quoting it since there are so many different versions of the bible's verses – and all the different denominations argue about which version is correct, but in 1 Peter 2:2 it uses the word 'babe' and in some versions, 'newborn.'

journey when we are quite young. Overcoming the mind and realizing that this whole story of *you* is a fictional story isn't an easy thing to do. Destroying who and what you think you are is not natural to being an organic being, but once it is done you don't die, you have to go on – life changes for you, you then see things much differently, everything gets much simpler, but watching everyone around you go crazy in their minds – that is hard to watch. What I am about to explain to you about the Wizard of Oz, I didn't learn from anywhere – it's just plain as the nose on your face, and as I explain it to you, you will realize this. My intention in explaining the allegory in this story is to show you that what I am saying in this book isn't new, but I want to use a newer story that is intended for our era because there are myriad stories meant to help us awaken. I'm not thinking that you will 'Wake Up' by my explaining this allegory, but only that you see how true it is that we have been laying down this breadcrumb trail since antiquity and that my message in this book isn't new, nor some theory I made up.

It isn't *which* story I use to demonstrate allegorical importance, but instead that I show how we have throughout history used allegory, and continue to use allegory, in many cases unconsciously – without realizing what we are doing. These stories are road maps, and are everywhere in the many cultures throughout the world, but we don't see them, or we fail to recognize them for what they are. The seriousness of our world situation is exemplified by our – many times unconscious – *obsession* to wake ourselves up to our true being – our singular and shared underlying consciousness. This simple children's story is – in my opinion – the quintessential example, the superlative delineation of the transcendental allegory – and importantly, it's contemporaneous to our time, and aimed at

## The Dream of the Mind.

the "young at heart." MGM didn't even follow the book precisely, yet the message is intact – which is the beauty of allegory.

**Wake Up!**

## The Wizard of OZ

The story starts out with Dorothy running down a dirt road, away from the camera, experiencing seemingly ordinary difficulties with life's mundane incidents, and one of those incidents happens to concern her closest attachment, namely: her dog, Toto.  Toto's importance in this allegory is that he represents that primitive, animal side of being human where intuition arises – the inner side that is unconscious to Dorothy. Toto walks bravely alongside her throughout the entire journey – she holds Toto significantly close, often carrying him because in the allegory he is an integral aspect of Dorothy.

We see Dorothy running down the road, *running away* from something, having to do with a Ms. Gulch.  A gulch is a ditch, or a ravine, or a canyon, which are excellent metaphors for an imposing obstacle.  It is significant that Dorothy is *supposed to be* about 12 years old – (although Judy Garland was 17 when they made the movie).  12 years is typically the age of being called on to use reason and common sense for oneself rather than relying on others.  She is at that age at which in some cultures (especially in older cultures) an initiation ritual takes place to symbolize the transition into adulthood.  Dorothy is at her wit's end because the obstacle, Ms. Gulch, wants to destroy Toto, which is Dorothy's inner confidence and intuition – you could even call Toto an integral part of Dorothy's inner self.  If you've ever read the book or seen the movie: 'The Golden Compass,' you could call Toto – Dorothy's 'Daemon.'

Allegory doesn't need to be tightly depictive or interpreted.  It must be loosely depicted or interpreted so that it can fit an individual's particular

# The Dream of the Mind.

situation. That is the beauty of allegory. The parables of Jesus are a good example – they are tailored so that anyone can find a particular parable meaningful in their own life. Our lives are all different which makes allegory the perfect platform for delivering a message that can be interpreted by the individual, and/or a collective group such as a family, or a community.


So... Dorothy is going about the farm seeking advice from the farmhands, Huck, who in Oz becomes the Scarecrow; Zeke, who in Oz becomes the Cowardly Lion; and Hickory, who in Oz is the Tin Man.

So, what's happening here is that before Dorothy goes to Oz she is seeking answers outside herself. This is what we do – instead of looking within ourselves for answers, we look to things outside of ourselves for answers – oftentimes, other people.

Our focus is outward – just as with Lot and his wife, in the story of Sodom and Gomorrah; They were leaving Sodom where people were identifying with their personal narrative (the mind) where wickedness abounded; Lot and his wife left the 'wickedness' (outward) path to seek out God (looking inward). Lot's wife *looked back* and was turned to salt – an element of many meanings metaphorically, but we all also know that salt eats away at things – destroys things. This exemplifies our need and unconscious desire to move inward – and once we do – *not to look back.*


Huck advises Dorothy that she needs 'brains.' Zeke advises her that she needs 'courage,' and Hickory advises her that she needs 'heart.'

Finding out what tools will be useful on one's journey to become

## Wake Up!

'aware' is far from being 'aware.' But... the story continues...

Dorothy's song, "Somewhere over the Rainbow" is relevant to the story, it belies Dorothy's *intuition* (precognition) that there is a place where everything is at peace, a true home, as well as Dorothy's *intent* to find this place: "that's where you'll find me."

Somewhere over the rainbow
Way up high
There's a land that I heard of
Once in a lullaby

Somewhere over the rainbow
Skies are blue
And the dreams that you dare to dream
Really do come true

Someday I'll wish upon a star
And Wake Up where the clouds are far behind me
Where trouble melts like lemon drops
Way above the chimney tops
That's where you'll find me

Somewhere over the rainbow bluebirds fly
Birds fly over the rainbow
Why then, oh why can't I?

If happy little bluebirds fly beyond the rainbow
Why ...oh why can't I?[19]

---

19 Somewhere Over the Rainbow, lyrics by E.Y. Harburg.

# The Dream of the Mind.

Dorothy's Uncle and Aunt Em are hardly able to help Dorothy at all. The best they offer is essentially, "I dunno Dorothy, guess yer gunna have to let ol' Ms. Gulch have her way and have Toto destroyed." So, Toto is handed over, but he quickly escapes and runs home to Dorothy. In other words... Dorothy's intuition, strength of character, and her confidence are not so easily undermined, and she manages to rescue herself, or escape from this attempt to destroy her inner strength and character.

So... Dorothy does what many people do. She runs away from home, and thus runs away from *her problems*. That usually helps... ...for about a minute. She soon runs into the old carnival mystic who takes her in; he sees through her self deception and sends her straight back home and into the heart of her storm. He tricks her and makes her think that Aunt Em (someone so close that she is an intimate part of her life) is having a heart (of the heart) problem; all due to Dorothy's own egotistical selfish irresponsibility of running away. Clever fellow – but then, he is an early representation of that magical side of the allegory, that person who Dorothy looks up to; before she gets to Oz – the carnival fortune teller, whom in Oz will become – The Wizard of Oz.[20]

Now keep in mind that this is a transcendent story (allegory) so it can't chronicle every little detail in Dorothy's life that has brought her to this point. It is enough information for the viewer to see that she is in distress, and there is conflict in her mind and that she is trying to find answers to understand and hopefully overcome what she sees as her problems and her

---

20 This motif of the trickster is the same as spoken of in American Indian mythology and spoken of at length by Joseph Campbell. Find it on Youtube.

failures.

She practically runs home. There is a storm brewing, and it's all around her, and *about her*. The whole story represents Dorothy. Every image in a transcendent dream is an aspect of the subject. Psychologist Carl Jung pointed out that every part of our dream is actually a part of us. Each character/person, and in many cases, the objects we see in a dream is not someone else, or something else – it is a part of us. With a symbolic dream, we are being handed a road map that has very strange and archetypal imagery that can be very eerie, sometimes outright scary.

There are some dreams that don't possess this primitive power. Some dreams, when we aren't yet sleeping too deeply are very coherent to us, while others during deep sleep have very strange and surreal imagery. It is the latter type of dream that is our road map. Unfortunately, most people don't remember their dreams – especially when the imagery is so surreal and cryptic that it doesn't make sense to them in the first place. And, when they do remember a dream, some folks go to a book about dream interpretation which isn't likely to help them. Dreams, and allegory in general, are specific to that particular person because that person has a particular narrative that they have developed over many years. While much of the symbolism in dreams can be common, those themes can mean very different things in context to the particular dream(er).

So, back to the saga... Dorothy hurries back to the farm to make sure Aunt Em is okay, and also because – for allegorical context – she has to face her demons, so to speak, and go into the storm. A Great Storm is brewing for Dorothy, and when she gets back to her farm she finds herself

# The Dream of the Mind.

alone, unable to get any support from anyone there. Aunt Em and Uncle Henry have taken shelter from a tornado coming in the distance, but for the sake of the allegory, Dorothy is abandoned, on her own, and she is now going into the heart of her storm. She has hit rock bottom and her only option is to turn inward – to accept her own demise, to die to who she was, and find her inner self. She is about to be 'reborn.'

It's important that we notice that this part of the story has all been in Black and White. This is significant allegorically because until we turn our focus inward our world is – relatively speaking – black and white, we get only occasional glimpses of the beauty that lies within. Until we turn within our world is the world of opposites – of which black and white is a strong representation. Excellent use of archetypal imagery here! Was MGM conscious of the genius of using black and white for allegorical purpose? As I have said, we do this unconsciously sometimes not realizing the genius of what we are doing.

So... Dorothy retreats to the safety of her bedroom (her innermost sanctuary), and gets conked on the head, and is knocked out. A dream begins in which the house (her house) is ripped from its foundations, and swept aloft in a whirlwind, the tornado.

Humans often use some version of the idiom: "Better keep your house in order." We are not referring to the an actual wooden or brick house that is your abode – we are referring to the person; who they are, and what is their inner state. Your body and mind being your house. So, again the allegory is following the transcendent theme.

# Wake Up!

The house lands with a thump, now in OZ.

Now we are in OZ, and Dorothy is in the land of her psyche. She will now experience the mystical. Oneness: that which is mystical, possesses a magical quality.

The house lands in OZ and Dorothy makes her way outside. When she opens the door (to her journey inward) everything is in vivid color. The Wizard of OZ was one of the first movies to be broadcast in color. Color helped the allegory.

Dorothy ventures out into Munchkin Land and is marveled by the beauty of her surroundings. She explores – everything is representative of an aspect of oneself in the transcendent dream. Many times in the transcendent dream there is a guide. The guide is another aspect of oneself, but the mind still is the projector for this dream, and has *some* – not as much – but *some* influence in the dream... ...and the mind believing itself to be separate won't accept that awareness can be discovered without the help of something else – *something other* – a guide. So sometimes we give ourself a guide. We don't need a guide, but as long as we believe our self to be the individual, the other, we will believe that our higher power is something other – so some folks will conveniently give them-self a guide when having transcendent experiences, and some folks won't feel they need a guide – it's all very subjective, and different for each person. If you've read Carlos Castaneda's books you will remember how important a guide was to Don Juan and Carlos Castaneda. Many Native American stories also incorporate a guide such as a coyote, or an eagle, or some other animal that that individual identifies with.

Dorothy's guide, Glinda, arrives as a floating bubble. This is quite

# The Dream of the Mind.

appropriate to transcendent allegory because a circle is a symbol of wholeness. Glinda is the Good Witch of the North. North is the Meridian; the Midheaven, the open sky, the direction we see in our maps as up – up is toward the light. North is eternal solid ground. Glinda informs Dorothy that Glinda has come because the Munchkins have called Glinda because – it seems – "a new Witch (Dorothy) has dropped a house on the Wicked Witch of the East."

The East is the rising sun – the morning of our life. It is significant that the journey starts in the East and moves West to the setting sun – the evening of our life – *and the Wicked Witch of the West is what must be overcome.* The East is Birth, Springtime; the West – Death, Winter. So our journey through life is from East to West – allegorically, and in some sense literally. It's not a coincidence that we call the Western World: "West." The Western World: Europe, the United States... is seen as the more progressive, open-minded, moving forward, not being stagnant or backward.

Witches are magical people – people of magical qualities. In most stories, witches are of the evil ilk, but we also have seen many good witches in our fairy tales and folklore. So, Dorothy, now that she is in Oz, is acknowledged as a person of magical quality. We are all witches (magical people) in the sense that we all possess the power to self-realization. Dorothy is still unaware of her own magical qualities. Glinda asks Dorothy: "Are you a good witch or a bad witch?"

# Wake Up!

Dorothy explains to Glinda that she is not a witch at all; just an ordinary girl from Kansas, an ordinary place, and that she just wants to find her way back home. As we all know she is directed to seek out the help of the all-powerful Wizard of Oz who resides in The Emerald City. At this point, if you are getting the hang of this, you know that the Wizard of Oz would be – at least in Dorothy's mind – that omniscient, omnipresent, omnipotent entity we think of as your higher power, whatever that might be to you: your God;  and you should see that the Emerald City is that place where your higher power/God resides.  Dorothy does not yet realize that her power and potential lie within – not in some Wizard or Emerald City.

To get to the Emerald City, Dorothy must follow the Yellow Brick Road (the Golden Road).  Golden objects are used very often in stories of transcendence to exemplify that which is of the highest value to us; even today, there are superstitious belief's that deify gold, which is indicative of why gold's value is not only inherently monetary but has a much deeper significance in the human psyche.

After much pomp, ceremony, and fanfare from the Munckins, (The little "Welcome to Oz" musical), Dorothy is sent off on her inward journey down her Golden Road to her goal, the Emerald City, her place of self-realization.  The journey inward does not begin in realization; realization comes only after much contemplation, and for the time being Dorothy is still thinking that she will find her higher self outside of her – in something 'other.'

BUT... she is not allowed to continue without one very important item.  Glinda transfers to Dorothy's feet the ruby slippers (the slippers were silver in the book, which has a significance in that silver is a pure

# The Dream of the Mind.

metal and intrinsic to purity – whereas the rubies are gems, but in either case – both are items of great value). The slippers are important to the allegory here because they show continuity, in the form of footsteps. Dorothy is continuing her journey which started way before Oz. This is very important to notice: The Wicked Witch of the East is Dorothy – Dorothy's old self – which is now dead, killed by Dorothy herself, and her new self, the "new witch" being Dorothy, has moved from outward to inward. The shoes (footsteps) move from the old self to the new self, and the journey continues except that now it's an inward journey.

This is what is meant in the Bible and elsewhere by being reborn, or 'born again.' Many Christians think it means to be baptized, and/or, that it means the point in your life where you accept Christ as your Lord and Savior – but reborn is actually when you move from outward-focused to inward-focused. The Munchkins (an inner aspect of Dorothy) even verify that the old self (the Wicked Witch of the East) is really (indisputably) dead, an authentication of Dorothy's rebirth and that this is an actual transcendence, a dying of the outward, and a true movement inward – not just a superficial attempt or egotistical sham.

The Wicked Witch of the West makes her appearance here, and warns Dorothy that she will never complete her journey and will succumb to her fear, insecurities, and of being inadequate; i.e., she will not be able to overcome her mind. The Wicked Witch of the West tells Dorothy: "*Those shoes belong to me, only I know how to use them; I will get you my pretty, and that little dog of yours too.*" The Witch of the West represents that part of Dorothy – Dorothy's shadow side – that must be accepted and

99

assimilated. It cannot be ignored or cast off. It must be acknowledged and faced fully as part of Dorothy. It is that part of us that we abhor – the side of the spectrum that we call darkness, the side we want to reject, but fully a part of the spectrum of what and who we are. It must be embraced as part of who we are – it CANNOT be ignored or rejected – it will not be discarded; if you reject it, or try to discard it you will not Wake Up. Without embracing it, and assimilating it into a part of who you are, you will not succeed and you will be haunted by that part of you. The Wicked Witch of the West is that side of Dorothy (of each of us) that is fear, distrust, anger, hatred, lust, perversion, our insecurities, inadequacies, and all of those "wicked" qualities that humans reject and refuse to acknowledge as fully one half of who we are. And that part of Dorothy lies not only within her, but until she accepts it and assimilates it, it lays before her, in the West (the future) – the direction that she has no option but to travel – one way or the other. Will awareness come to us or not, is our own personal dilemma; do we Wake Up, or not – that is the conundrum.

After the Witch of the West leaves, Glinda admonishes Dorothy to not let the shoes leave her feet or she will be at the mercy of the Witch of the West, i.e., Once you start your journey inward, Don't Look Back!. Dorothy then sets off down the Yellow Brick Road with proper goodbyes and fanfare from the Munchkins.

She soon meets up with the Scarecrow, Tin Man, and the Lion who represent her understanding and need for a brain (wisdom and intelligence), heart (strength and compassion), and courage (bravery and resilience) necessary for a journey inward, but to symbolize Dorothy's insecurities and inadequacies, the Scarecrow is a scatterbrain, the Tin Man is hollow, and the Lion is a coward.

# The Dream of the Mind.

A few obstacles are thrown in her way – enough to make the point that such a journey has many perils. Perhaps this part of the story is underdeveloped (it's a movie, and can't be overly long), but she gets to OZ and gets to see the Wizard – her first glimpse of what in her mind she feels is her goal. She asks for his help in reaching her goal – of getting home. She is hoping to be recognized for demonstrating wisdom, compassion, courage, and for how well she has done in regard to her inward journey thus far, but the Wizard – apart from scaring the crap out of her – just tells her that to prove her worthiness she must kill the Witch of the West, and bring him her broomstick. The broomstick to the Witch of the West represents the Witch's power. The broomstick transports the witch, just as the ruby slippers transport Dorothy. Dorothy is sent packing... ...gotta get that broomstick – somehow.

In other words, Dorothy has not yet confronted and assimilated her alter-ego.[21] Humans, and some animals that possess higher brain function, have an unrelenting habit of repressing unwanted feelings. When I use the term alter-ego this is what I am referring to – that part of oneself that one does not want to express or, even admit existence of – that other part of you that stays hidden. This is the biggest challenge that humans face in the move to awareness – an unwillingness to admit to, and then to embrace, that part of you that you have rejected. I don't remember where, but I have read of it referred to as a bag that one carries around on ones back in which one tosses feelings from unwanted experiences or unwanted thoughts, and that when the bag becomes full... things – ugly things – start to seep out.[22] It's only the mind that causes these things to end up in the

---

21 By alter-ego I do not imply dissociative identity disorder.
22 I think it may have been in a book by author Robert Bly titled: "Iron John."

bag to begin with – as Shakespeare so rightfully stated in Hamlet: "There is nothing either good or bad, but your thinking makes it so." This is absolutely 100% correct. The same thought is echoed in Milton's Paradise Lost: "The mind is its own place, and in itself can make a heaven of hell, a hell of heaven."

The desire to return home is the desire to be reconnected to our true self, which is pure consciousness – which is oneness, which is all that we are. We know we are oneness, but we can't remember, yet we do intuit it. We want nothing more than to be reconnected with it, but our mind wants us to think that it is complicated when it is actually quite simple. We make up all these myths and allegories to help us find our way – little road maps, but it is extremely rare that a person becomes realized before death.

Dorothy has approached the doorstep without first merging into the awareness of her entirety – her wholeness. She must accept her whole being; those parts that are in the shadow as well as those in the light. Every naughty, disgusting, nasty, ugly part of us must dangle on the mobile that represents who we are – and all must dangle in the light. All parts of us are necessary, they are all valuable. It is all of our parts that have made us who we are. Dorothy must accept as legitimate all aspects of herself that she had previously refused to allow into her conscious thinking. All of those naughty, nasty, dirty, lustful, loathing, hateful thoughts that we automatically reject and refuse to talk about are very real and legitimate thoughts that we must discuss, and in some way allow expression in our life. Remember the Shakespeare quote that nothing is either good or bad, but that it's your thinking that makes it so. All of the

## The Dream of the Mind.

skeletons in our closet must come out of the closet and hang on the clothesline in our front yard for all to see. We must accept, express, and talk about them because we will not be whole until we do, and you will never Wake Up until you become whole.

So, Dorothy is sent back to the haunted forest (the dark place) where she must find and kill the Witch of the West, (assimilate all aspects of her). In this allegory, this results in the death of the Witch of the West and requires possession of the broomstick (the Witch's power), but this act assumes the death of the Witch. Either Dorothy must die – which would mean that Dorothy has failed in her inward journey, or the Witch dies which would translate into success for Dorothy, assimilation of that part of herself that was rejected/hidden, and thus becoming whole.

The journey westward continues – the West being the setting Sun – toward one's destiny. Along the way, in the haunted forest, her courage, brains, and heart fail her which is illustrated in the haunted forest when her compatriots all run away in fright or get pulled apart as what happened to the Scarecrow, and Dorothy is spirited away by the henchmen of the Witch – the flying monkeys, who take Dorothy to the Witches castle – the Witches fortress. In other words, the journey inward is fraught with uncertainty and peril. We chicken out, or said more truthfully: we give in to the tricks of our mind.

The Witch gives Dorothy an ultimatum: Give up the ruby slippers (Dorothy's power), or the Witch will kill her, and her little dog, Toto. Of course, Dorothy knows that the Witch will kill her whether she gives up the slippers or not – allegorically this means that if Dorothy quits now she will have failed – which equates to spiritual death.

An aspect of the Witch is her representation of those parts of us that doubt, fear, and prevent us from letting go and dying to *Oneness*. It is the mind (ego) that wants to exist forever, and the mind (ego) is a narrative – not even real. For Dorothy, that narrative is the story of Dorothy Gale – the character in the story. Just think about yourself, what's your name? Where did you get that name? Who gave it to you? Who were you before that? You were alive in your mother's womb; who were you when you were in the womb? And now, not only are you that person who goes by your name, but you also think that all your experiences are part of that definition of who you call yourself. That is your identity, your ego, which exists only in your mind as your own personal little narrative. And that narrative stored in your brain, which your mind has convinced you that you are, wants DESPERATELY to survive. A frantic attempt by the mind to exist beyond the grave.

If you suddenly found yourself unable to remember anything you wouldn't be dead. Who would you be then? Sure, you might be in the loony bin which is why we need the mind and our brain to store our memories to survive in this world, but who would you be if suddenly you lost all of your memory. I can tell you that all of your family, friends, and doctors would be showing you pictures and telling you the narrative of that person who you – supposedly – were before you lost your memory. They would be trying to restore you to the narrative that *they* understood you to be, and something might click and your memory might be restored, but if your memory wasn't restored you would still slowly start to become the narrative they were giving you even though you couldn't remember. You wouldn't be able to fill in all the missing pieces, but you would be able to add to it future experiences, and that would be fulfilling enough for you to start over. You could also pick a new name and start over, but either way, you would need to fit in, you would desire to fit in, to be a part of the collective – the community.

But... you do need your mind to survive in this world. The trick is to be able to use the mind, but not identify with it, i.e."to be in the world, but not of the world."


Dorothy goes into a panic and cries out for help to Aunt Em and Aunt Em replies through the Crystal Ball; Aunt Em, another aspect of Dorothy calls out to Dorothy: "Dorothy, where are you? We are trying to find you." When a person truly makes up their mind to make the journey home, to go inward and break the cycle of egotistical rationalizing, every ounce of the inner self pushes in the effort to reach the goal. Here, that intuitive side that seeks awareness: the Oneness, breaks through and tells Dorothy: "we're trying to find you." The intent is for each and every one of us who is lost in the *dream of the mind* to not give up; look within; don't look back; die to the world; Wake Up!

Here in the dark fortress of the Witch of the West, in the depths of despair and hopelessness, when all is lost, and life seems like it's about to end, Dorothy regains her brains, heart, and courage illustrated by the return of the Scarecrow, Tin Man, and Lion, with Toto. Remember that Toto escaped from the Witch of the West, and went and found them, and led them to Dorothy. Dorothy's own determination and fortitude (Toto) brought them back. Our own determination and fortitude can win the day and bring us back to our senses. Many suicides happen at this point.


So, the Tin Man, Lion, and Scarecrow sneak back to Dorothy and (her brains, heart, and courage) free her from the place she was locked up (where she was stuck). It's easy to get stuck when we are making the journey back to our home; back to being aware of what and who we really are; awareness that our mind is only a narrative – a story.

Freed, Dorothy is pursued by the Witch of the West who represents our shadow side, that part of us we don't want to own – yet must own; trying to keep us in fear and doubt, to keep us from awakening from the dream of the mind – our mind trying to be infinite. She finally catches Dorothy in a castle tower and orders her to hand over the ruby slippers – once and for all. The Witch threatens to destroy Dorothy, but not before destroying her friends – which implies that the Witch will defeat Dorothy's courage, heart, and brains first. But when the witch lights the Scarecrow on fire Dorothy grabs a bucket of water. Water is one of the most basic elements and can represent life, death, change, rebirth, and renewal, to name a few. In this instance, it allegorically represents spirit, transcendence, rebirth, and renewal – a washing away of illusion.[23] Dorothy throws the water at the Scarecrow to put out the flames but inadvertently splashes it onto the Witch of the West who then *melts*. She melts into nothingness. Dorothy liquidates her! The Witch melts into Dorothy – so to speak.

Through an act similar to baptism Dorothy assimilates that part of her that has been missing since conception. She comes to terms with her doubt, her fear, her inadequacies. She faces the reality of her nakedness; that knowledge represented by the Tree of Knowledge – at birth, as our narrative developed, and we learned of our naked vulnerability. An absence of our connection with *Oneness* (free will) causes all of this

---

23 In the Bible water is known to represent the Word of God. How powerful!

# The Dream of the Mind.

mayhem, delusion, and the dystopia we experience.

Dorothy is presented with the Witch's broomstick and all the Witch's minions bow to Dorothy – all of the Witch's powers, properties, possessions, and strengths go to Dorothy. (This story is so rich with allegory.) She heads back to the Emerald City to get the Wizard to take her home. She is confident of her ability to go home now, she possesses the broomstick, but she still thinks that something "other" is going to get her there. So... back to the Emerald City she goes. Notice though that awakening is not instantaneous when Dorothy becomes whole. She still thinks that something greater than her is going to perform some miraculous thing to awaken her – to bring her home. Humans have pastors and priests, gurus, roshi, shamans, and saviors, and here, ... a wizard.

This time when she meets the Wizard, Toto pulls the curtain back and reveals that it's just an ordinary man *pulling strings*, creating the illusion of an almighty and powerful Wizard of Oz. This action of unmasking the ordinariness of the Wizard allegorically operates to vaporize the notion of the Wizard/Savior – which is tantamount to liquidating him as she liquidated the Wicked Witch, and by liquidation, they simply melt into part of Dorothy and are no longer considered by Dorothy as something separate from her that she needs to find – thus, she becomes her own Savior... ...as it should be... ...what you seek is within.

Those aspects of Dorothy she has been unsure of are thus recognized and validated: (wisdom) the Scarecrow gets his honorary degree of ThD, the tin man gets his heart (fortitude), and the lion gets a medal for bravery(courage). But, he has nothing in his bag to magically transport Dorothy home because what Dorothy has been seeking – her *Oneness* with all that is – she has possessed all along though she has not quite yet fully grasped it. The mind is very tricky, and although Dorothy has vaporized the belief she had that he was a place where she could find the answers to life, she still thinks that this ordinary man is a Savior who can get her home. Toto pulled away the curtain (veil), but she is still stumbling... the mind is very tricky.

I think it's very true to form that the Wizard (which Dorothy thinks of as her Savior that will bring her full circle back to *Oneness* – her home) employs a hot air balloon to transport Dorothy back to Kansas. A balloon is an ordinary thing that uses basic non-magical components and is – ironically – just a bunch of hot air. The move back to *Oneness* requires transcendent qualities... ...what we consider as humans to be magical qualities, and the Wizard and his balloon don't have any magical qualities, so it's no surprise that this method fails. The Wizard whimsically departs Oz in blundering fashion. Thus the notion of the Wizard/Savior is fully exposed as a hoax, and the Savior layer of the delusion drifts away on the wind.

Dorothy starts crying and her brainy Scarecrow friend comforts her, and her other senses (all the characters of the dream) all assure her that they will love her. But, alas here comes Glinda in true *magical* bubble fashion to save the day. Glinda is only a guide, not a Savior. There is no Savior for any of us as much as many folks would like to believe – except in the sense that you are your own Savior. You don't need saving, but your mind can't allow you to believe that – it can't be true because if it were then all of the reasoning, and rationalizing, and the glitter that the mind has thought up would be worthless, nothing but a narrative – nothing more than a spectre – a ghost. And in that sense, ghosts do exist as spectres of the mind. Your mind and identity is the real ghost. Identifying

# The Dream of the Mind.

with the mind is a *delusion*.

Dorothy asks Glinda: "Can you help me get back to Kansas?" and Glinda tells Dorothy that she doesn't need any help, that she has always had the power to go home to Kansas. The Scarecrow asks Glinda why Glinda had not told this to Dorothy before and Glinda answers that Dorothy had to learn it herself – which is what we all must do ourself; *Oneness* cannot be understood – it must be experienced. This is Glinda's magic, and this is true magic, but remember that Glinda is only a guide. The magic to bring ourself to realization is always within us. We all have to learn it by ourself – it can't be proven; Jesus used parables to guide people; we continue to use allegory which is essentially the same.

The Tin Man then asks Dorothy what did you learn? to which Dorothy delivers the most important line in the whole story. Dorothy says that it wasn't enough to just want to be with those people she loved, but that "*if I ever go searching for my heart's desire, I won't look any further than my own back yard, because if it isn't there, then **I never lost it to begin with**.*" Dorothy had to seek the answer within herself; "What did you learn?" is a question to cause one to reflect – to look within.

Our heart's desire is to find our contentment. But, as long as we are seeking that happiness (better termed as 'contentment') in the world, in those things outside of us, we will never be content – not truly content. Contentment, true contentment (which we conflate with happiness and/or joy) lies within. You may think that you have found it in the dreamy eyes of your lover, or your daughter, or your son, but you only see in them, a reflection of what is within you. You may think you have found peace and harmony in the birds and trees in the forest, but you only see a reflection of what is within you – you only see a reflection of *Oneness* – which is what you are, what you have always been, and what you will always be. Looking for your splendor in things outside of yourself may get you a taste of that which you seek, but it is ephemeral. This is what is meant by Dorothy's statement, "I won't go looking any further than my own back yard." Your back yard is that which is within you... right there... in the back – behind your mind. If you don't find that which you seek within you, then what you seek isn't real to begin with.

Glinda tells Dorothy that the Ruby Slippers can now take her home. That which has faithfully moved Dorothy on her inward journey, her own footsteps in which she walks, the Ruby Slippers, which came to Dorothy when her journey turned inward, can now deliver her.

Dorothy then wakes up in her bed back in Kansas. Dorothy's statement: "There's no place like home" is a testament to having truly come home to the truth of who you are and what you are.

Very important here is to understand that her journey didn't result in Dorothy ending up in some sort of heaven or nirvana... what it resulted in is Dorothy's firm and solid placement 'in the world,' but no longer 'of the world.' She has become aware of her *Oneness;* her ordeal has caused her to Wake Up from the Dream of the Mind.

This is a truly amazing allegory and movie. It comes to us at a time when the world is coming into deep division, and during the industrial age as we start racing toward self-annihilation. When the book first came out it was interpreted in a political/economic allegorical schema which is pretty crazy, but ... not in atypical fashion for the *dream of the mind.* The mind wants to turn anything and everything it can into a product that

# The Dream of the Mind.

serves the interest of the mind, and politics and economics are creations of the mind. This movie was huge, a blockbuster like no other; it is still shown on network television every year; this is because we all can sense its import. Despite the fact that most people misinterpret this story, they intuit its significance. With regard to any misinterpretations, this story is not a collective allegory to be interpreted at the social level; it's a personal allegory to be interpreted at a personal level. It's your Storm, your Ruby Slippers, your Yellow Brick Road, your Glinda, your Wicked Witch, your Emerald City; it's your journey.

I chose not to cover every element of the Oz allegory such as the Munchkins, or the field of poppies which are important, but I have broken this down more than I probably need to, and you should be able to derive meaning from the elements of any story at this point. They may have slightly different meanings for different people depending on your experience. The poppies to me are a representation of our tendency to addiction (poppies/heroin), and/or our wanting to numb ourselves to the tremendous difficulties of life, and of overcoming the mind – our wanting to give up, give in, or just go to sleep which is synonymous with being in the dream of the mind.

I've not elaborated extensively on every little nuance of this story because the minutia of it can be argued, and we should focus on the overall message, and not the minutia. You should be able to intuit these elements now. I just wanted to give you the main gist of the allegory so that you can now understand it, and find the elements of all the magical things you have in your life that are there for you – to guide you.

These elements of the transcendent journey are present in all good allegories of transcendence. What the transcendent story tells us is that we

111

must confront and assimilate all of who we are as an individual living on the material plane: good, bad, ugly, and accept those things that we have done, or have failed to do – everything – and then acknowledge that none of it was wasted, nor was it ever real – it was just a story, a narrative that we became so mesmerized by... ...that we were hypnotized by it to the point of identifying with it. It doesn't matter how good we were, or how bad we were – we simply did those things, and now we see that the character that we thought we were, that we thought was our identity was never real to begin with… it is an illusion and not real – just an actor in a play, and that we have always had what we needed, but just didn't see it before.

It's sad that Judy Garland played this role, sang that song, but didn't get it... was so unhappy, and died lonely, and depressed. But, nobody got it, so who could tell her?


There are so many movies that are allegorical and/or analogies to our awakening that I can't talk about them all, yet there is one recent movie that I want to point to. *The Matrix,* though not a transcendent allegory is a superlative analogy of our misidentification with our mind. You might find in it transcendent elements that apply to you, but I don't see this movie as a *model* of transcendent allegory. This movie stars Keanu Reeves who plays a character named Neo, and Samual Jackson who plays a character named Morpheus. This movie is not particularly useful for illustrating the transcendent movement from outer to inner vision, but instead, this movie illustrates through an analogy with virtual reality technology that the mind projects an illusion. This movie builds upon a theme in which the world is ruled by machines which use computer

# The Dream of the Mind.

technology to create a virtual world (A Matrix) where the minds of humans are sedated, and placated in a virtual reality, while their bodies are used to create electricity. In this story, the world humans exist in, and experience is virtual – computer-generated, while their bodies lie in suspended animation in a pod-like device.

The movie starts with Neo, a computer geek and hacker living inside of the virtual reality called: The Matrix. He is suffering from a deep feeling that things are not as they seem – that there is more to reality than what he is experiencing. He sees some ambiguous glitches in his computer screen (intuition) and sees the name Morpheus in several command-line messages. He then meets a woman named Trinity at a party, and Trinity tells Neo that she can set up a meeting with Morpheus – which she does. He then rendevous' with Trinity who takes him to meet Morpheus. First Morpheus tells Neo: "Unfortunately, no one can be told what the Matrix is – you have to experience it for yourself." As I have said previously: *Oneness* cannot be understood, it must be experienced. In Greek mythology, Morpheus was the God of Dreams (of Sleep), and in this movie, the theme is that everyone is asleep to the truth of the Matrix. Trinity is the 3 aspects of God (Father = Oneness; Son = The Individual or that which is 'Other' such as people, and all that is physical; Holy Ghost = Transcendence) in most mysticism, and Neo means New – *(The Initiate). We are so good at this stuff !!!* ...and don't even know it.

Morpheus then offers Neo a choice between 2 pills with the caveat: "take the blue pill – the story ends – you wake up in your bed and believe whatever you want to believe; take the red pill and you stay in wonderland, and I show you how deep the rabbit hole goes." Little to say, Neo takes the red pill and *wakes up* in a pod that resembles a seedlike 'pod', and he's immersed in water – which has amniotic/embryonic symbolism. Plenty of metaphorical/allegorical stuff going on here, and much of it leaning toward the transcendent. Once again: rebirth. Neo becomes aware that the world he had lived in all of his life (his identity) was just an illusion – a virtual world.

In this particular story, those who have awoken by taking the red pill are able to inject themselves back into the virtual world using something akin to a scary-looking USB blade that plugs into the back of their neck and slides into their brain stem. They are able to live in the virtual world without being of it, yet if they die while in the virtual world, they also die in their underlying reality, but... near the end of the movie Neo becomes 'enlightened' and realizes that those who have died in the real world after dying in the matrix was only due to *lack of faith.* He then faces his own death while in the matrix and is *resurrected.* At this point, you should catch the inferences for the lack of faith and resurrection. In my opinion, this movie does NOT delineate the path to awareness; the journey inward; the movement from seeing oneself as an individual to seeing only one single self (Oneness). In my opinion, the Matrix is an *analogy* of the human dilemma… believing the mind to be our true identity – of living in a virtual reality (The Dream of the Mind). The Wizard of Oz, on the other hand, has all of the elements of being lost, finding the inward path, assimilating all elements of oneself including one's demons; and finally the journey home to Oneness.

The Matrix is an illusion inside of a delusion. Instead of being once removed from the truth, it is twice removed. After Neo takes the red pill and wakes up from the illusion of the matrix he is now in the delusion of *the dream of the mind.* Now he is a regular human identifying with his mind as who and what he *thinks* he is. But regardless, the Matrix is a

# The Dream of the Mind.

great analogy for *how* we are fooled.

In the movie Avatar we are pointed to the underlying truth that we are all one. The planet and everything that exists is all a part of who, or what we are. Another metaphor, but not a movie that shows how to get there.

The 2015 movie "Lucy" is another allusion to the fact that we are all 'one' and that we are everywhere all at once. This story isn't true to the transcendental journey either, but it does allude to our being more than just this body and at the end of the movie there is the allusion to Lucy becoming one with all that is which is slightly backwards because we don't become one with all that is... ...we already are one with all that is – it is only our lack of awareness to that fact.

Another contemporary story is Star Wars in which Luke Skywalker becomes a Jedi Knight and uses *the Force* to battle the forces of evil. This story isn't the best allegorically because, in my opinion, the minutia is excessive, so I won't go into details, but it's still a signpost and should be seen that way. The Star Wars movie involves a battle between good and evil (represented in this story as "the force" and "the dark side.") which is absolutely incorrect. There is no "battle" happening between good and evil except relative to the mind's eye. What we are actually dealing with is more of a struggle to become aware – and the mind has created an illusion – the narrative.

Crazy thing about it is that our only tool to overcome the mind is by using the mind. We have to go through, not around. The mind must concede to itself. In *The Matrix,* there is also a battle happening that, at first, might seem to be between good and evil, but if you look more closely, what Neo wants is to wake everyone up, i.e., the effort in 'The Matrix' is to wake everyone up to the illusion of the matrix – the matrix being the illusion. That is correct! The Matrix provides an analogy of the illusion rather than an allegory of transcending it.

There are several sequels to *The Matrix*, but after the first Matrix movie the analogy is lost. As I said previously: The Matrix isn't true to the transcendent allegory, but is an interesting *analogy* to the illusion we are trapped in.

The only battle between good and evil happens within the individual in the effort to reconcile the light and shadow (good vs. evil) sides of his/her humanity. And these sides must be reconciled – which is a real **battle** (a very difficult struggle) for most all people.

A while back I spoke of how we have evolved our brain and mind because on the physical plane we have to survive. It's important to note that all of the bugs, animals, plant life, and all that exists on the physical plane have evolved to survive. A gnat has no less part to play in this elegant dance than you or I. We are all part of a whole – don't let this fact slip your awareness. The wolves need the deer. The deer need the grass. The mosquito's kill off those animals that become vulnerable to the mosquito. Mosquitoes can get a virus too, or become bird food. And believe it or not, the deer actually need the wolves too. There are viruses, germs, parasites, and predators, that all have their purpose. The Earth is a very elegant and fragile ecosystem that needs ALL of its various parts, and it's always in flux; in other words, it's constantly evolving and changing; species come and species go. It's a great symphony that we call life. From one comes many, yet the many are but one.

All animals have a mind. An insect has a mind just as a mammal, but the smaller the brain or central nervous system the less cognitive ability.

# The Dream of the Mind.

Bacteria have less mind than insects, but they all have minds. They do things that require choice. Watch dogs as they compete for dominance. Watch other animals – they all compete, they all make choices. They all encounter obstacles and find solutions – even ants and bacteria encounter obstacles and find solutions. They all have brains to store experience and memory, nervous systems that work as the electrical grid connecting it all together, and the electrical field that brings it all to life, and allows the connections to seem simultaneous and/or instantaneous.

But it is humans that have the most ego (mind). Humans – like mosquitoes or fleas – will kill their host without any thought of allowing the host to replenish itself. Humans will destroy the earth before they will conform themselves to living in a harmonious symbiotic relationship with the earth. Humans are parasites when they live in the dream of the mind – they have no self-restraint. It's not like we have no choice but to destroy our habitat – *the **choice** is ours*. The Mosquitoes can devastate the animal population... but then the Mosquito will no longer have a food source and will die off, and the animals will rebound. If not the Mosquito then something else, a virus, or who knows until it happens. *Oneness* (in this particular context, "Nature") will always provide a solution to an imbalance in the animal population. Each species does its part to keep the system in check, but only in a limited manner. The Moose get too plentiful, the Moose get taken out by some parasite, or virus, or some other malady. But, humans, because of our intelligence, we find countermeasures to Nature's attempts to take us out, and consequently look at what we are doing: destroying the entire ecosystem to such a degree that it could be catastrophic to the entire planet. Nevertheless, when the Earth shudders the humans will die; *Oneness* will prevail... some species will rebound – and even a few humans will likely survive in some corner of the world.

The lower you go on the organic totem pole the more attuned to awareness that particular animal or organism is. The higher on the totem pole the less attuned to awareness the particular animal or organism is. Humans are the most intelligent, but the least aware – the more mind, the less awareness, and vice-versa, the less mind, the more awareness. Mosquito's are more aware than humans. Watch the mayfly. It mates and goes to die – no fear, no anxiety, no need to fear or be anxious. Intelligence has nothing to do with it. It's not that you need to know what awareness is before you can attain it. Awareness simply 'is' – you don't attain it. You already are it; it is your mind that prevents you from being in that awareness. The transcendent allegories don't show you how to get there as much as they tell you that you're already there. It is a process of 'awakening,' not becoming knowledgeable.

I will liken it to this: *Oneness* puts on the costume of "the mayfly;" then, when the show is over *Oneness* simply sheds the costume, and that's it. The costume goes into the recycle bin, and breaks down into its constituent atoms that recombine into something else that is apropos to the place and moment. It's not a bad thing, it simply "is." No worries!

Humans actually want drama. They like to think. They like to think that they are important. The mind is obsessed with building and adding to the narrative. We want to have more, or we hurt someone else's feelings to make us feel better. We hate worrying so much, but we work assiduously to create things to worry about.

# The Dream of the Mind.

But the punch line is that all of the drama and story-line that we want so badly to be real is nothing compared to that which *'is'* ...that which 'is' is without drama and story-line. Keeping oneself in awareness of *Oneness* is far more calm and peaceful, balanced and serene, than any of the angels and heavenly goodness narrative, with hell and its atrocities. Angels and individual souls, and heaven and hell, are inventions of the mind, devices created by the human mind to sustain the mind, but utter folly compared to *Oneness* of that which 'is.' Find the reality – it is within you as all that is – in this moment. It 'is.' I am!

## Oneness and Good & Evil

Getting back to what I stated earlier: Shakespeare, in Hamlet, said it quite correctly: "for there is nothing either good or bad, but thinking makes it so." And in the same way, you create your own heaven or your own hell by what you think. While we are living in this physical world the play of opposites exists. Heaven and Hell are not some ethereal thing or place; they both are states of *mind*. That's the only place they exist: *in the mind*. If we removed humans from the playing field there would be no heaven or hell, there would be no good or evil. These things are mind things on the conceptual level. Without humans there is no heaven and no hell.

We think of light as the good side of the spectrum – such as: "go into the light;" and we think of darkness as the evil side – "that person is in a very dark place." It is to some extent necessary to make these distinctions, but they are not in and of themselves true. We must define things to live in the world, and some of those things that we define may not be pleasant for us, so we have labeled them and given them definition according to their application and implication. When things are pleasant and make us happy they fall more on the side of what we consider good, or perhaps even heavenly; and when they are unpleasant on the side of what we consider bad, evil, or even hellish. Good and Evil are relative, and we need to understand the nature of why some things happen the way they do that makes them unpleasant rather than negate them and attempt to eliminate them from the world of experience. Such a result (eliminating them) is not only impossible – but insane. All parts constitute the whole. It's ironic, although somewhat predictive of our labeling paradigm that in

# The Dream of the Mind.

the English language we have taken a letter out of good to become god, and added a letter to evil to become devil. (Good = God), and (Evil = Devil). How convenient!

We MUST learn to not judge or condemn because if we do then we necessarily judge and condemn our own physical existence. Those things we think of as evil cannot be eliminated any more than those things we think are good because they are part and parcel of the same thing – two sides of a spectrum, the front and the back. So how do we, as a collective, reconcile these polarities?

We all share what Psychologist Carl Jung called "collective consciousness." Jung found that people in remote places on opposite ends of the earth who have never had any sort of contact – these two separate societies shared the same symbolism and archetypes in their dreams. He also found that there are different levels of collective consciousness. For example, our *family* is a very small, yet very real unit of collective consciousness. Our families are tightly-knit units; you often know what other members of your family are thinking and feeling without them even telling you. Our neighborhood is another; our town, another; our State or Country another; our planet, another. Each smaller one is a sub-collective of the larger. The larger the collective the less *personal* the connectedness. But, just because it's not as personal doesn't make it any less significant in the bigger picture.

Often, for some reason, we will know exactly what someone else is feeling, or we might know what they are going to say before they say it. We do share our consciousness. We are all really the same thing, so how could we not? *Oneness* is the vibration that we all arise from, and it is not our fault that we don't bring this memory with us when we are born.

# Wake Up!

Unfortunately, we have no place to store the memory of the Oneness before we are born. A brain is necessary to store a memory, and before we developed a brain in the womb we didn't have any physical storage device, so it is no surprise that we didn't bring any memories with us when we moved into existence in the physical world. But, we do bring consciousness with us – how could we not... ...*Oneness* (consciousness) is all there really is, and we are it. However contradictory it may sound you are the whole thing – not just a piece of it. In this physical world, you may think you are "other" than it; you may think that you are one small piece of it, but that's not correct. *Oneness* is singular. It's just one thing, and you are it. Even though you are seemingly separate, ...you aren't *really* separate. You are part of the single awareness. That sounds contradictory! ..."*part*" of a single awareness, yet you are the whole thing. Language is the problem – it's like language is useless to convey this message, except... we gotta get there, and words are what we have to work with.

The sentence: "you are *part of* a single awareness" is correct, but it's relative to existence on the material plane. Explicitly, you are not *part of* a single awareness; you are the whole thing. On the material plane, it just doesn't make sense. What causes the illusion of separateness is a narrative that is created by your experiences, education, fear, bias, judgments, etc. – all of which exist only in your *mind.*

As the boiling point of water is reached (100 degrees Celsius or 212 degrees Fahrenheit), water vapor starts to form inside the liquid in the form of bubbles; they rise to the top, and they grow bigger as they rise just as our narrative (ego) grows bigger as we age, but the bubbles are never separate from the water. If they had a brain and memory they would think that they were individual bubbles for that brief period of their existence, but then they would reach the top and pop and become what they were in the first place again: the water, only now – because of the heat – in the form of water vapor.


Oneness is omnipresent: in everything, and everywhere all at once. So, being that we are life bubbling forth from it, we can intuit it. We know it's there, but can't see it, or prove its existence. We know we are it, but can't prove it. That's just how it is. That is the secret of the mysticism that we have all been trying to fathom, but coming up short. That is the reason for all of the allegories that we have created as our breadcrumb trail to help us find home.

We **must** recognize that we share this consciousness. We have a responsibility to recognize our shared consciousness. We have to understand that we are all brothers and sisters in this game we call life because if we don't humanity is in terrible trouble. We want nothing to do with that which we see as evil, but we are as much evil as we are good.

When you feel emotions, good or bad, they bleed out of you into everything – into all things, and especially into other people and animals. Emotions cause vibration and people share vibrational frequencies.

Everything that exists in the physical world can pick up on it, but things of the same frequencies are more attuned to each other's vibrations. Your frustration can turn into someone else's frustration. Your calmness can make someone else calm, and your happiness can make someone else happy. The more harmony we feel the more harmony we will have – not necessarily in us as an individual, but in our world; the more disharmony we feel the more disharmony we will have – not necessarily in us as an individual, but in our world. When you keep things bottled up they go into the metaphorical "bag" that you carry them around in, but *they escape*.

We've all heard this one a million times: "You reap what you sow." It doesn't just apply to your actions. It also applies to the energy you put out. You've heard people say that you seem nervous, or that you seem anxious, or that you seem like you are angry, or calm, or happy, or any other emotional state. Sometimes you can see it visually in the person's face, or in their demeanor, but some people are good at hiding their feelings, yet you can still sense it if you are intuitive. People can feel it, or sense it, because your energy is not contained within you. It is a very real *field* of energy, and we all share that field – it can move and travel, it's a vibration that reverberates through and in all things – it's like a chorus and we are all singing.

What I am about to say next is VERY important for ALL of us to understand, but also almost impossible to believe as true.

When someone goes out and starts shooting everything up, we are ALL responsible for it - **equally**. When the collective (society) is suffering a lot of frustration and anger – it comes out in ways that scare the shit out of us!

Maybe *you* can keep *your* cool, and it doesn't manifest through *you* personally, but that anger, that frustration **MUST** become conscious, it **MUST** find expression. We will feel it, but we can't *only* feel it, it must also be given expression – it has to manifest. If it were possible for all of us to be successful at suppressing it; if we make it our societal mission to try to repress it, then, when it does find an opening – a crack in our armor, a crack in the cosmic egg, then it will come out *savagely,* and with incredible force; the same would be true if we were able to suppress the skin lesions from measles and the illness continued to fester inside our body, the virus in the blood continued to multiply. When it did – eventually – find a weakness in the suppressing element it would come out with such force and intensity that it would certainly cause us to be aghast at what we saw in the mirror, if not simply cause us to die.

Most people work hard to keep feelings and emotions from getting out – afraid of allowing others to see how they are feeling. Some of us can manage our feelings better at certain times, but some folks have been having a harder time with their life, and are experiencing more inner turmoil, and are therefore more susceptible to emotional outbursts. *These folks are like lightning rods for the collective anger, the collective frustration, and they become the focal point for its expression.*

This is a constant of *Oneness*:

## *All feelings become manifest.*

Feelings are things of the mind that are similar to my analogy of the lesions caused by measles. Feelings start from thoughts in the mind, and if not quickly resolved, or reconciled, in the mind, they will become manifest just as spots on the skin appear when you have the measles. Minor feelings whether an irritation or a pleasure can manifest simply as a slight quiver, a twitch, or as a smile, but as the intensity of feeling increases, they can rise to a level where they manifest more intensely as a headache, sickness, or ebullient joy, laughter, etc. Laughter is a way of burning (resolving) feeling such as a minor embarrassment or a minor joy, just as crying is a way of burning away feelings of sorrow and despair.

Feelings unresolved can increase into some form of action or inaction – if not through you, then through someone else who is less able to suppress their feeling(s) than you are, and that person has the potential to become a lightning rod for the vibrational frequency that we humans share – that collective consciousness.

This is easier to observe in the smaller collective unit – the family. Dad might come home really irritated; he might take out his anger on the rest of the family, soon everyone is irritated. Then, the explosion might come from the child who is less consciously able to control his/her anger. Feelings can also manifest in the form of sickness or disease. Feelings can manifest quickly depending on intensity, so it's important to try to resolve negative feelings quickly. If not resolved, frustration builds, and those feelings will eventually manifest – sometimes in an explosion. Resolving them means to allow them to manifest in some way.

In the same way that it is easier to observe the sharing for feelings in the smaller collective such as family, it is harder to observe this in the larger collectives. It is not always that the feelings that cause this come from only one person. Since many people may be angry and frustrated, there is always plenty of this energy radiating out into our collective repository. It has always been a huge mistake to not realize that our feelings are subtly shared. With this knowledge and consideration, we can make a tremendous impact on our society.

Currently, almost 8 billion people are living on our planet. A majority of these folks are disenfranchised in one way or the other making for a lot of stress and tension.

The energy created by our feelings can be transferred. It happens in the collective. In a church, there might be a certain feeling and vibe happening that is being shared and transferred. In a group of protesters, a different energy is created. When we're alone we might be the only one feeling how we feel, but we will carry those feelings out of our room and house, and they will get transferred and shared because of our energy. This may happen in a small group of people or a huge gathering, and it can also bleed out from disparate individuals, groups, or other influences, and over long distances.

This is a result of the fact that there *Oneness* (Vibration) underlies all of the sub-vibrations that make up all of the individuals, groups, and all **seemingly** *other* things.

There is only one thing – *Oneness*. There are sub-vibrations of Oneness, but they are all part of the whole.

You might say: 'It can't be that way – it just can't be, what a nightmare that would be if it were true.

Well... It is true! It is never debatable – it's true. And yes, it is a nightmare. That's why we call something terrible a nightmare: ...because a nightmare is a type of dream, and we are living in a dream that can become a nightmare – the dream of the mind, the dream that we are an individual; a narrative apart from all that is 'other.' Originally I was thinking of titling this book: "Wake Up!"

We make stories and movies to show us, such as 'A Nightmare on Elm Street,' where a dream leaks out into the real world. ...but... that's *just* a movie... ...not a message, right?

We want to point our finger at that individual who shot up the school, or the shopping mall, and say: "he did it," but that's not quite true; he pulled the trigger, but we all had a hand in it. Our culture is all about the individual. We care about what "I" have, what I did, what I feel, and if others don't have what they need we rationalize that it is because they aren't working hard enough, or that they aren't asking for help in the right places. And if they shoot things up it was them – not us. It was "you," not "me." Well... have you noticed that the more we get this way, the more self-centered we become, the more egocentric we get – the more we see what I'm talking about – the more violence we see in our communities. All you have to do is look. It's plain as the nose on your face. And if you think that you don't have anger and frustration because you have a good job and take good care of your family, and all that other good stuff you do – let me ask you this: Do you get angry and frustrated about the kid who took the gun to school and killed his classmates? You are frustrated by all the violence – are you not? If you can't simply forgive – **instantly** – then, **you contribute!** Forgiving is an instantaneous resolution of feeling. Not forgiving is to carry that anger, resentment, and other feelings.

As I pointed out: when someone has the measles it causes spots on the skin as the disease develops. The spots on the skin are the indicator to us that we have a virus inside of our body that is making us sick. If we pay attention to the spots we can identify the sickness and seek a solution – a cure. Besides forewarning us that we are in peril, it also forewarns others to stay away. The spots are the messenger – you can't cure measles by putting make-up on the spots so you can't see them – *don't shoot the*

# The Dream of the Mind.

*messenger.* Violence in our communities is an indicator that our society is sick – not an individual(s) as we like to think, but all of us, and it's also an indicator to others outside our community to stay away. We can't cure the sickness by singling out the shooter and putting them in jail – that's the same as treating the symptoms of measles, or killing the messenger – that will just make matters worse – we're not addressing the actual problem! We can't cure symptoms without curing the cause. We may find some aspirin to relieve symptoms but to resolve the symptoms we must resolve the underlying cause.

Our own collective mental illness is finding its **necessary** expression through the mayhem, shootings, terrorist acts, etc – to wake us up to the fact that we are suffering this collective illness – this mind vomit. It is a very real and deliberate message we are delivering to ourselves. If we don't want to recognize the message and address the problem; if we just want to be in denial of it... well... *enjoy THAT ride!!!*

But regardless... you are a part of the problem instead of the solution if you don't recognize our *Oneness* – if you don't *Wake Up.* When we go after the virus instead of the spots on the skin then we can cure the underlying issue, and then the violence and mayhem will stop all by itself. It will take a while, but the pendulum will slowly swing back.


***All feelings become manifest.*** You might think: 'well... I felt really angry at so-and-so, but I didn't act it out,' or I felt this, or I felt that, and it didn't manifest.

...Yes, it did – just in a manner that you didn't, or haven't noticed, or it didn't manifest through *you.* Scary thought, isn't it... Funny thing is that

# Wake Up!

it's not that people don't realize this, it's that they refuse to accept it, they don't want to admit any responsibility.  IT'S NOT ME!!!


One slip, and down the hole we fall
It seems to take no time at all
A momentary lapse of reason
That binds a life for life
A small regret, you won't forget,
There'll be no sleep in here tonight [24]


You walk into a room and say: "Wow, the peacefulness in this room is incredible – You can feel it!"  Or, you may feel a great amount of love in a certain group of people.  Of course you can feel it, it's real, and it's apparent without anyone saying anything.

But it goes both ways.  You can just as easily walk into a room and you might say: "Wow, you can feel the tension in this room – you could cut it with a knife."  Well, of course you can feel the tension. Feelings are part of our collective consciousness.  You walk into another room and might say: "Wow, there is a lot of anger in here."  Of course you notice it, because our feelings are all shared in the collective.  We share them! And, some people are better lightning rods to pick up those feelings than others. It can be particularly frustrating to pick up on negative feelings, but not know what they are coming from – what happened to cause them. Someone who carries a lot of anger and resentment is more likely to be a receptor for the collective frustration and anger, more likely to be that

---

24 A small excerpt from a Pink Floyd song taken out of context, but it could just as easily be talking about the dream of the mind – *the narrative.*

# The Dream of the Mind.

lightning rod, and sometimes more likely to act on it.

We all have known that we should: "Love one another," "Do unto others as you would have them do unto you," "Give and you will receive," "Love your enemies as you love yourself," "Judge not, that you may not be judged."

These are just a very few truths (maxims) that we already know. I think that a lot of the reason we don't apply these more in our personal lives is because we haven't understood the magnitude of the ramifications for not applying them. *We are one – yet many, but when we see the many – remember that we are one.* This is so very important! We want the harmony, but we are working harder than ever to be separate from one another; I want mine and you get your own – beat it! Harmony requires unison – we must all sing together... ...and always with the careful introspection as to whether we are singing in harmony, or if our song is dissonant.

Nothing we do to stop the mayhem and chaos will work out for us except for understanding that we are one single thing, and must therefore act accordingly – working together in a collective effort recognizing our *Oneness* and staying awake to that. More police won't help, more rules won't help.

We can't apply make-up to the spots on our skin and make the measles go away. We must treat our collective society as a unified whole – as a single body united, and as a planet we must be united; and on the smaller collective level of being human we must be united. We all share the same underlying consciousness, and there is NOTHING we can do to undo that.

131

# Wake Up!

We can't invent our way out of it. We have no choice but to recognize this and come into unity, or we will suffer the consequences of whatever hell our minds can dream up – and you have seen how horrifically creative our minds can be in movies and television shows. Soon it won't be some children in some far off school being shot up, or some far away concert venue, it will be up-close and personal – and the police won't come and help you, ...eventually, it will be the police and/or soldiers who will be the ones doing the killing. If we don't Wake Up we will sink deeper and deeper into our own created hell. Our own Nightmare on Elm Street.

Most people are all about self preservation, while I am all about self sacrifice. That makes me a poor businessman – lol. When I discuss my poor business model with people they almost always say to me in one form or another: "That's not the way the world works." This is one of those phrases where words are monsters. In actuality, what they mean to say is: "That's not the way this world operates." For the world does work through generosity, love, and self sacrifice, but it operates through greed, corruption, and self preservation. This, of course is the recipe for our own destruction – and we all see that happening all around us everyday. It's a contradiction in terms to say that our societal systems "work" (as in they 'operate functionally'), when they are not functioning very well at all – although... some societal systems function better than others.

Some people say that we can't possibly come together and be one. "That's impossible!!!" ....No, it isn't impossible. It's just that people keep saying it's impossible. It is true though that we can't all come together as one all at once; it happens one person at a time. It has a snowball effect – the more who Wake Up the faster others will awaken – it happens exponentially. This book is intended to expedite the process.

## The Dream of the Mind.

So, what are YOU going to do about it? That is *the* question, and that is the *only* question.

A while ago I said: "So how do we as a collective reconcile these polarities?" You might have thought as you continued reading that I was implying that we can't stop the mayhem that occurs and that we must therefore just accept that it is going to happen regardless of what we do, but I wasn't implying that per-se. What I did say quite clearly was that we cause these things by what we think, and through the feelings created by those thoughts; for it is thoughts that cause the resultant feelings. When one side of the spectrum improves, the other side corresponds accordingly. It balances! It will always balance – might take a little while, but it will always balance. The pendulum will always swing back. The same correlation can be made with the amount of anger, frustration, anxiety, etc., we have in our society: It balances! The amount of violence we have in our community is directly correlated to how disenfranchised people feel; how angry they are; how fed up they are, how much anxiety they have about where their next meal will come from, or where they can sleep, etc.

This is how we reconcile these polarities. If we want less mayhem we adjust our thoughts to quit being so angry, frustrated, and resentful. And if that anger is caused by, lets say... that we have nothing to eat while others have more food than they need, then those people who have more need to do more to share. As part of the 'one' we need to watch and pay attention to all the other parts of the 'one' that exist within our range of community and reduce stress wherever needed as best we can, to the best of our ability – to adjust the harmony of our song. If there are too many people to feed, then we should quit making babies as though babies are a validation to being a normal acceptable female. We need to change habits such as watching television so much, and quit making entertainment with violent content exciting, alluring, to the point that daring young individuals want to emulate it – the Jason Bourne character is an excellent example of what many young people want to emulate. It's alright to make these shadow side movies, but if we overemphasize the shadow side then the balance is offset to the shadow side.

These are only a couple of examples of the things we can do. Touching upon women having babies is not going to be a very popular example, but it is true that if there are too many people we should make less – it is a *choice* that we have – especially in the age of contraceptives. I'm not talking about purity or puritanism either. There is also some truth to women desiring to have a baby as a given right. They may have the womb and freedom to get pregnant, but in the early months of 2020 with nearly 8,000,000,000+ human beings on the planet, having children on a whim, because we can, is not exactly a choice made wisely. We know what is good for us as a whole, as a collective, and what is not good for us – you only need look inward to find the answer to any question.

We actually promote our mayhem. For example: News shows show more violence and mayhem stories because people *want* to hear about that type of news. We are unwittingly feeding the mayhem. In other words, we must understand that to see the murders on the news we need perps to do the murdering, or stealing, or raping, etc. – there *is* a correlation! Supply and demand. If we all buy a certain product, more of that product will be produced. We all know this, so why do we keep purchasing mayhem? And if we want to keep purchasing mayhem – which is what we must want (or we wouldn't keep doing it) – then why would we

# The Dream of the Mind.

complain when our society produces it for us? – think about it... if the news channels know that more violence grows the audience, and they show more violence for this reason, and the amount of actual violence grows in our society, then why would we complain about it when *we are the ones watching it, and coincidentally making it grow* – not just on television, but in our communities.

The networks know that more sordid content will attract more viewers, more viewers mean more advertisers during popular – violent, or what we call 'mature' – content, more advertisers mean more revenue, and the ratings have proven that we enjoy seeing sordid/violent content. Sounds twisted ...and it is, but it is also true. We say we don't want to see anyone get hurt, but we enjoy a movie in which we watch as people are being hurt, or even killed, as long as it's not "real," and not us, or our family, or someone close to us. Well... it gets real ...real fast! What we think so we get. Ask, and you shall receive.

We are asking for it – people turn on the news because they want to know what's happening in their community, but they are mainly interested in the crime that has happened. The news channels show us some happy things, and we like to see *some* happy things because it relieves our conscience of the guilt of enjoying the bad news, it makes us feel better to see some happy things, but the broadcasters know that they generate a bigger audience if they show ugly news. And we do all of this because it generates more money. Generate more wealth – that is the general idea. More entitlement. We cry and complain that we don't want our children to get shot up at school, or at a concert, or a sporting event, yet we work feverishly, although unwittingly, to make it happen!

I mean... is it possible that we might be responsible for this? **I'm**

# Wake Up!

**being sarcastic – of course we are responsible!** We can't say it was the elephants – they caused this, or it was the lady bugs – they did it, or the trees, or the rocks. And it wasn't the perp any more than it was us – we are equally responsible – each and every one of us. Just Google: "Violence on television makes more money," and you will get enough articles to have you reading for hours. It's insane! Mind vomit – yet each person wants to make the same argument: "It wasn't "*me*."

Hey... I know... lets put a liquor store on every corner and a gun store across the street from the liquor store. Lol... ...but only in the impoverished neighborhoods.

How do we adjust our thoughts to quit being so angry, frustrated, and resentful? Not that long ago, many communities, or tribes of people would dress up in animal skins or paint themselves to represent the shadow side of our human psyche, and they would dance and perform rituals to express this animal nature and/or the shadow/dark side of the mind. The entire tribe or community had to attend this ritual. All members had to participate. This was done to act it out, so that it didn't manifest in an unwanted way. Ancient people personified the shadow side of the psyche as deities, demons; gods and goddesses, witches, and every sort of magical entity. Throughout history humans have consigned the complex parts of the psyche to a far away place; for example, we have put the gods in the heavens, and the dark elements hidden deep down in our psyche – below our conscious awareness. We did this less in ancient times, moreso in modern times. Modern society must find a viable way to bring the shadow side to the surface because it *must* manifest in some way – and if we resist... ...well, ...good luck with that!!!

We must recognize that we are all one single thing. We are all connected. *Oneness* is all that exists. We are that. I "am," and ...I am that ...and that ...and that. When I look in your eyes I only see myself looking back. When we accept our responsibility for our part in the collective *Oneness*, then that harmony will become manifest not just in our individual life, but our collective life as well. By becoming aligned with *Oneness* we will do less harm, and we will do what's right naturally, without any special effort.

Physicist David Bohm who is well known for his interest in consciousness has said: "Reality is an undivided wholeness...a new notion of unbroken wholeness which denies the classical analyzability of the world into separately and independently existing parts...The inseparable quantum interconnectedness of the whole universe is the fundamental reality."

There is only one thing, a singular thing – in itself and of itself. Calling *Oneness* "God" is a terrible label to use because it denotes something 'other.' "God" denotes an anthropomorphic quality; our mind wants God to be an individual similar to our image – a body of some sort. Prior to the 20th century the label "God" was used because people didn't understand quantum physics, particles, atoms, molecules, and the cells that make up our bodies and the elements that make up the world around us. Now, through science, we understand the world around us, and the term "God" is no longer a necessary label. It's outdated and useless. It worked for primitive people... ...and it is still used by 21st century people who are bound-up in primitive thinking – folks who identify with their mind as who and what they are.

Don't wait for the next person to Wake Up. It is with each person that awakens that it becomes easier for the next person. Your task is a personal responsibility to Wake Up. We do have individual responsibilities, but they are relative. Don't allow the illusion of the individual sink you deeper into a personal identity.

All these people who are the lightning rods who we have condemned to whatever hell we have consigned them – they must be reintegrated into our communities. We are all – every one of us – responsible. We are unable to cut a part of ourself away. Even those we don't like are a part of the whole. Some people think that "God" is going to come along and save us from ourselves. This misconception is flawed: One, it recognizes that we need saving which is demonstrative that we know perfectly well that what we are doing is contrary to *Oneness*. But more importantly: Two, it is recognized that *Oneness* is omnipresent, in all things at all times, which substantiates the fact that *Oneness* doesn't need to come or go anywhere to save anything when *Oneness* is already here – present in everything. Since we are *Oneness*, and since *Oneness* is all that is... how can *Oneness* come along and save *Oneness*?

And if you have made it this far in this book then you know... we must Wake Up!!! – and I'm shaking the tree!

Way back in the first pages of this book I told you that the story of Jesus actually completes an allegory that was started in the Old Testament.

In the old testament the Jews relationship with God was governed by the Law; the people had to obey the Law (of God) to be "saved." In the old testament the connection with God was lost, (remember the Story of the Garden of Eden). The old testament relates to us the outward vision of living in the world and being of the world.

So before Jesus (Old Testament) there is a loss of connection, a loss of

# The Dream of the Mind.

understanding, which must be overcome by action – obeying, understanding, and getting to know the rules of the game.

Jung calls this "Shadow work." Implicit in this is being able to align the innate shadow side (sinner) with the innate light side. *You must be good* (follow the rules) *despite the fact that you are not inherently good.* Of course, you aren't inherently bad – you are just as much good, but you must align these two sides – this dichotomy of human nature. A better way to say this in our current time-period would be to say that you must learn to stay balanced and not lean too much in either direction, e.g., *You can kill something to eat it, or use it for good reasons, but not for reckless reasons.* You are a steward of the Earth, but – more accurately – a steward of *Oneness*.

Then the story of Jesus tells us the story of a man who transcends earthly limitations and is one with God – the "Son of God." Jesus takes us over the rainbow. Jesus tells us overtly that we are all God's children – that the kingdom of God is "within."[25] *"If I ever go looking for my heart's desire, I won't look any further than my own back yard."*

The journey turns inward. We are all the sons and daughter's of God – we are all one with that which 'is.' With the story of Jesus we come full circle back to the awareness, or unification, with that which 'is': *Oneness*. We are all the sons and daughters of *Oneness*. We are in the world, but NOT of the world. Jesus is the turning inward and seeing the *Oneness* that we all are, that we all share. God's son – one with God. With the Jesus allegory we see an actual death and resurrection. A *transfiguration*.

In the Wizard of Oz we see Dorothy's turning inward in the beginning

---

25 -Luke 17:21

when she gets conked on the head and passes out, i.e., a life in crisis that causes a turning inward: that which we seek is within, and that we mustn't reject any part of ourself regardless of any shame we feel, or hurt, or fear, and – in fact – we must assimilate all those undesired feelings and acknowledge our bad actions and accept those things, and thus return to wholeness which is necessary before we can die to our ego, and return to *Oneness*. The allegory of Jesus involves an actual person who actually lived, and is more literal in its imagery of death and rebirth which brings us to the final step in the inward journey: *death to ego, or rebirth, transfiguration, and the return to Oneness.*

But, lacking for me in the Jesus allegory is that we must accept all of our psyche; there is nothing we can reject; all parts of us are a *legitimate* part of us, which make up the whole person, or better said: which makes the person whole – this is another point in which the Wizard of Oz becomes the better allegory.

There is what I consider to be an interesting element in the Biblical allegory that is not in other allegories that I know of. It is important to the allegory and important to understand. Jesus becomes hated by the very people that he represents – the Jews. The Jews might say that he didn't represent them, but what he didn't represent was their version of the God story.

Once again... the Jewish collective story; the Jewish narrative; the Jewish *mind and collective ego* didn't like Jesus' *mind and ego*. He was a Jewish Rabbi, and he was a Jew, so he was representative of the Jewish tradition and culture, except that Jesus was a mystic. The Jews – his own people – turned against him. Then they asked the Romans to arrest him. Then they voted to crucify Jesus rather than Barabbas. By putting

# The Dream of the Mind.

Barabbas above Jesus they unwittingly lowered Jesus to 'lower than common criminal status.' This is metaphorically significant because by lowering Jesus to 'lower' than common criminal status – it puts Jesus in the metaphorical position to represent everyone, not only the "worthy," (whatever worthy means), but the unworthy as well. This is important because there is only *Oneness,* and none are ever left out. So, before they reject and kill him – and they reject him quite violently, – and in so doing they make him the metaphorical redeemer for all. That, seems to me, is very significant to this allegory.

Then there is the death and resurrection – of a real person. This allegory includes a real life person. Jesus overcomes death. Now we have life everlasting in the literal sense. This is hardly the first time in an allegory/myth/legend where a hero gets resurrected from the dead. Right about here people are going to start screaming: "How can he say its an allegory? Jesus was a real person, he really lived, the story is true." This may be true, but I have also pointed out that sometimes allegories are built upon real lives and situations. More importantly, we tailor – even – actual events to suit the need of how we want a message perceived. Yes... we will twist a story; hide facts; and even lie. But... ultimately, it is the only *Oneness* which is leading the – mystical – orchestra, not some individual(s). Even though the facts were hidden and the story twisted, as much as the Catholic Church has tried to control the Bible throughout history; with all their genius, power, and clever artifice, they failed to touch the mystical message contained within. Their focus was on manipulating the message in its literal sense, so the mystical message survived. But, in 1964 the Gnostic Gospels were found providing a side door into the mystical and original story of Jesus. This has been quite controversial for the church.    The most logical course of action for the church to take is to simply refute the Gnostic Gospels as hypocrisy and rubbish – which is exactly what the Church has done.

The resurrection is the return to Oneness, the becoming again of that which you always were – *rebirth*.  As I said, You were never born and you will never die.  The life of Jesus, from the virgin birth to the  resurrection is the ultimate metaphor for never being born (the virgin birth), and never dying, (the resurrection).


I'm getting into dangerous territory here.  Jesus was born like anyone else – coitus.  And he died, and his bones are somewhere hidden away. But, the entire story is an allegory – and a *very* good one – and sculpted by us, but unwitting to us is that the allegory we were sculpting was actually coming from deep within our consciousness.  We unwittingly knew exactly – precisely – what we were doing.  We all build up the allegorical. We all try to become the hero, or that character that we venerate.

I know...   ...this is hypocrisy, and it's antithetical, and I should probably be burned at the stake, but the traditional and conventional story of Jesus isn't helping us at all due to the fact that it is taken and interpreted literally – the mystical is negated as heresy.  We need to get ourself out of the mess we're in, and to get out of that mess we need to Wake Up to the lies and BS that has been fed into our minds since antiquity – and to do that all that is required is to quit identifying with our mind – with our personal narrative.


The story of Jesus is an interesting story.  Jesus was an aware person

# The Dream of the Mind.

who knew that we are all one with God. Jesus' message and story was limited by his time-period and the knowledge people possessed at that time. There was no quantum physics or higher mathematics at that time. He had to work within an entirely different framework. His stories and parables were relative to the time-period and told in a manner that was understandable to the people who lived during that time-period. He worked with what was available, and because he had to deliver his message in person he had to be somewhat elusive, or cryptic, about the message. Something that Jesus couldn't do is put it out there the way I am doing in this book; had he, he would have had his ass handed to him long before he did. He couldn't write a book and put it in the stores. I guess he could have just written it all down, but there were no publishers, and I don't think that parchment and writing utensils were readily available at a local store – and he certainly didn't have a computer. He did become more and more overt in his message in his final years knowing that he was walking the plank with the sharks waiting below. He knew he was going to be killed, and he even talked about it with his followers. Crucified, on a wooden cross... 'a dead tree with its arms sticking out to the sides like branches.' The Tree of....

There is no doubt that a man named Jesus who had extraordinary wisdom walked this earth, but what really transpired in those more questionable moments is not known. We do know that the church has benefited greatly from its version of the story as it is *taught* by the church, and considering the churches influence during the first and most of the second millenniums, it's utterly phenomenal the way the allegory has survived, and it's only because it was cryptic metaphorically that the crux of the message is preserved allegorically. The Church only changed the story in its literal context not realizing that it was the allegory all along that held the true message. The Church tried assiduously to make the allegory fit into the dream of the mind – our delusional contorted invention of who and what we are – rather than finding the hidden meaning of the allegory.

We also know that many of the records (gospels they were called) were hidden away, such as the gospels of St. Thomas, Mary Magdelene, Judas, Phillip, and many others, (these are called the Gnostic[26] Gospels), and only found recently. It's a pity that they were hidden, or some people might say they were – mysteriously – lost. But... it is certainly understandable why they 'mysteriously' ended up misplaced since they convey the mystical point of view. We also know that the gospels were not written until – in many cases – after the writer was very old or dead. They say that Jesus died around the year 30 and that the synoptic gospel of Mark was written in about 50 AD, then Matthew and Luke in about the year 70 AD, and the gospel of John in about 80 AD. I'm not going to try to dispute the history. It makes no difference, but it shows a huge gap in writing down what these men considered to be the most momentous event in their lives, and – religiously – in all of history. Why would they wait so long to write down what they considered the most important event in history? (History... remember that history is just 'memories' of changes). Perhaps they were writing the entire time and were just *very* slow writers. We also know that the Catholic Church exclusively controlled the Bible for the first thousand years after it was written, and the Church had exclusive access to that book, made any copies that needed to be made, and made any changes that they felt were... umm… necessary.

---

26 Gnostic, derived from 'Gnosis' meaning: knowledge of spiritual mysteries.

# The Dream of the Mind.

I don't want to argue the details – especially with this particular story/event. The mind likes detail because the more detail – the more the mind can go off on every tangent as to why such and such is wrong; the "I'm right, but you're wrong arguments." Power... look at the divisions in the church... Power. Give people a little intelligence, and its mind boggling how much pain, suffering, and sheer terror they will inflict on one another!

How is this allegorical when Jesus was an actual person, and not a metaphor in a fictional story.

Allegory doesn't need to be fashioned from fiction alone because *Oneness is all that exists.* Whether the lesson comes from what we consider real life situations, or from stories we create – it makes no difference. Both form of lesson come from the same *Oneness.* We think that we as individuals are the creators of the latter form of allegory: stories that we create, but it is only the mind which insists that we are individuals in the first place.

We intuit that which exists underlying our physical realm – *Oneness.* We are compelled to become aware, and we are always moving in that direction to some degree. If we want our life to unfold in a certain way we will make it unfold in that way – even if it happens subconsciously. We sometimes call this the power of positive thinking, sometimes the power of suggestion, and sometimes we attribute it to prayer. If we want someone else's life to unfold in a certain way we can make efforts to set events into motion to make that happen the best we can – a manipulation, even if we do so subconsciously. If we want our environment to be shaped in some certain way we can make efforts to make it happen – even if we do so subconsciously. In our minds we may all disagree about making something happen, yet we may subconsciously make it happen anyway, or we may cause something that we don't want to happen to not happen – and we may do it subconsciously. We can also undermine all of our best intentions by thinking negatively. We do this all the time, and all human events are shaped by our thinking and resulting intention – even Jesus' life and death. Sure, Jesus had the biggest part in how his life unfolded, but every member of the community are contributors and shapers to each others lives.

So we come into this world naked (vulnerable) and without any memory of the *Oneness* from which we came. We end up trapped by our mind, and need knowledge to survive. We store knowledge and information in our brain, but we don't have any memory of what we were before we were born because we couldn't start storing memories until after we had a brain to store them. We accumulate vast information in our memory which amounts to nothing more than a huge narrative that we identify with, and think/believe that we are that narrative. We are lost to our divinity and our *Oneness* – we can't remember anything before the narrative began at birth. We become the actor of our narrative.


All the world's a stage,
And all the men and women merely players;
They have their exits and their entrances,
And one man in his time plays many parts...[27]


Then, very slowly, we begin to awaken to our inability to find the

---

27 William Shakespeare from his poem: "All the world's a stage."

answers we need in the physical world. Our intuition can sense a missing part of us. Often, we look for that missing part in another person, our mate, or our children. People eventually turn inward to find that which they are missing, and then, if they are very lucky, they begin to realize that they never lost it to begin with. This book should help with that a great deal.

The life and death of Jesus completes the biblical allegory. Jesus is the denouement of that particular allegory. Jesus denotes the resurrection from the death of the narrative; the rise from the ashes; the realization of *Oneness* where the many become one; that which is lost and then found.

Perhaps by my not getting into a crapload of minutia, critics may just say that this book is rubbish because I don't have the 'erudition,' or perhaps because I don't address all of the great knowledge of the scholars (*which is mostly mind vomit; wind blowing across a parched desert),* or that I'm 'afraid' to talk about this in every possible tidbit of detail because I can't prove any of what I'm saying. Let me first say that NOBODY can prove, or disprove, the mystical parts of what is written about what we label the divine, … and I'm happy with saying only what I need to say and nothing more. Let the crows pick the bones! I do know though that the theologians will be compelled to rebuke this book – they have to, or they will lose their power.

## Eternity and One Magical Moment

Now it's time to tell you something that will sound even crazier. I have heard other notions of this, so perhaps I'm simply reiterating something that you may have heard before, but regardless, mathematicians will eventually put this together, and elegance will replace the incomplete picture physicists are currently working with.

### *There is no such thing as time.*

An unfortunate stumbling block for Einstein with regard to relativity was the inclusion of time as a factor. There is no such thing as time – there is only this moment. Time is an illusion. This moment is all there has ever been. If you close your eyes and meditate on that innermost part of you – that silence deep within, you will find that it's the same silent place that you knew of when you were a child – it's the same place at any point in your life. The only difference is the change you see occurring in the physical world – as it occurs in this moment.

I don't like having to be the one to point out an error by Einstein. I bet some people will be like: "Who does this guy think he is!" Well... I keep telling everyone who I am, and who you are, and what we all are... *pay attention.*

There is no time – there is only *change*. We *measure* the change that occurs in this moment, and compare it to our memories, and we call it time. People have learned to gauge time by watching the movement of the Sun, or should I say the movement of our planet. Then we split the changes we observe into segments, (years, days, hours, minutes, seconds), and call it time. I guess you can call those series of changes time, but then

# The Dream of the Mind.

you will be back in the illusion of time. There is only this moment. In this moment there is change. We measure the change and call it time. Simple. As stated, hopefully, it won't be too long before some quantum physicist works it out in the math, and then they will find that the math works elegantly.

If you were to think of the word 'time' as *change* and define it as such, then I guess it might have some validity, but if you think of time as a linear expanse which exists in its own space, (as it would need to if we were to think of time machines or time travel), then you are in a delusion of something that does not exist. Time is not some linear expanse as another floor of a building that we can make an elevator to get to. There is only change in this moment.

We often think that time is necessary for certain things to happen, but change continuously occurs, and change is all that is necessary. It seems to our mind that the moments we remember actually exist when actually they don't – not now, not in this moment, and this moment is all there is.

There is a British Physicist, Julian Barbour, who says essentially the same thing I'm saying with regard to there being no such thing as time: "As we live, we seem to move through a succession of Nows," says Barbour, "and the question is, what are they?" For Barbour each 'Now' is an arrangement of everything in the universe: "We have the strong impression that things have definite positions relative to each other. I aim to abstract away everything we cannot see (directly or indirectly) and simply keep this idea of many different things coexisting at once. There are simply the Nows, nothing more, nothing less." [28]

---

28 Popular Science Magazine, September 18, 2012

# Wake Up!

I did not get this idea from Barbour or anyone else. I did Google the concept of "no such thing as time" just now to see if anyone else has weighed in on this concept, and found this article by Barbour. There were some other hits too, but I needn't be distracted further – but more importantly – **you** needn't be distracted further; that's a big part of the problem is that everyone wants more explanation which is nothing but the mind wanting to make sense of it – and find fault. For the time being, ...understanding it more, figuring it out, is like 'chasing the wind.' Sooner than later, quantum mechanics will corroborate the fact that there is no such thing as time, but that can only be done through math and physics. People won't be able to understand it – it will always seem like there is time – but that's an illusion; there is change, and we measure change, and call it time. It's just one of those things that become apparent when you come to know your mind as a fiction. *There is no such thing as time,* just as the story that has developed during your life-time has no substance, the story that you have come to believe is real, the story that you believe is you; Time and your story have something in common: 'fiction.' Now is the moment – NOW Wake-Up!

Eternity is a word we think of as an endless time. We think of eternity as time never-ending, a interminable foreverness. There is only this moment and this moment is eternity. If eternity existed as an expanse of time then eternity would not be timeless; an expanse of time is measurable. We think of eternity as forever, but forever cannot exist in time, or it wouldn't be forever – unless you are confusing time with eternity?

Time is a quasi-measurable series of changes that you have in memory; eternity is not measurable. The concept *"series* of changes" also suggests a sequential expanse linearly, so perhaps a better way to say this

# The Dream of the Mind.

is: 'a list of memories that we have stored in our brain, and numbered as having occurred consecutively, sequentially, or in series.' With 'time' we think of a linear expanse. This is not the case. There is only one single moment: this moment. Changes do occur, and they seem to be sequential which provides the basis and foundation for the illusion we think of as time. If we think of time as only change that has occurred which we use as a tool to measure our movement in the moment, then time becomes a tool, but only a tool, and understood to be – only – relative to our need to keep track of changes that occur in the order they occur in – this understanding would be correct, and we would see time for what it is and what it is "not." I challenge you to show me another moment. Try... You will only be telling me about a memory, or... you will be *referring* to a memory, or memories.

I write these words right *now*, and you are reading them right *now*. This is what is meant by eternity. This moment is eternal. It simply 'is.' Remember... all that exists is *Oneness*. That's all that exists. You are *Oneness*, as am I, as is that rock, as is this moment. You are that single thing. We all exist within the *Oneness*, and as *Oneness* – all in this moment. *Eternity = Now,* and in the same concept: *The One appears as Many, yet the Many are but One.*

You might want to argue that dinosaur bones are evidence that time is real. No... dinosaur bones, and all fossils, are great evidence of change. Things come and things go... Actually, things simply *are*, and those things *'change'* – *in this moment.* The dinosaur bones *continue* to change – in this moment. Things come and things go... from the one come many, and the many are but one.

The mind makes so many arguments that time is real. Look at these pictures, look at the rust on my car... but the pictures are only relevant in this moment, and the image in the picture is what was in the moment – *this* moment to be factual. There is no other moment. There is no other moment when there wasn't rust on your car. There either isn't any rust in this moment, or there is rust in this moment. Things change ...in this moment.


Here is an interesting illustration. This isn't something that I am attesting to as fact; it is a thought that occurred to me, and it makes sense as an observation, and I think it's an interesting thought that may help to illustrate that things only change; that they don't go somewhere.

Imagine Earth long ago covered with water, and plant life, no humans yet, and far more plant life than animal life. We take this Earth and set it on a scale and weigh it. It weighs – for simplicity sake – let's say 100 pounds. Obviously, the Earth weighs much more than that, but I want to keep this simple. At first it is mostly plant life, but as the plant eaters grow in numbers, plant life is reduced while at the same time, animal life greatly increases. Plant eaters eat the plants, and predators eat the plant eaters, yum! Slowly the plants become fewer while the plant eaters and predators become greater in number. Eventually humans evolve, and as they grow in numbers, the numbers of animals, whales, fish, buffalo, elephants, lions, etc., all of the animals become greatly reduced because people kill them all, and sometimes just for fun – "sport" they call it. Same happens with the plant life. Humans start farming and using lumber, and the forests disappear even faster, yet the human population grows exponentially, until – where are we at now... close to 8 billion humans. At the same time nothing has left the Earth except a few satellites that

# The Dream of the Mind.

don't amount to much on the grand scale. We may have lost a small bit of our atmosphere to solar wind, but we have also accumulated countless asteroids, but the asteroids are foreign objects that are extraneous to this hypothesis, and asteroids and space dust would only amount to an infinitesimal amount to the size of the earth. Nothing substantial came, (not counting asteroids), and nothing substantial left, (except maybe a small bit of atmosphere, and some metal and plastic that we made satellites with). So, the Earth should still weigh very close to its original 100 pounds (not counting the asteroids). I theorize that it does!.

What has happened is that life has simply changed. The life force that was in the plant life has transformed, and now exists in the form of animal life – particularly human life.

Someone might argue that humans and organic life have a higher density and therefore the Earth does weigh more now, but then water would come into play because organic life, and particularly animal life, is made of mostly water – so therefore the oceans would have become a diminishing factor in such an equation. Change occurs – and it tends to prefer the evolutionary process to move toward higher forms of consciousness – which is precisely what is the intent of *Oneness*. When humans came along (evolved) they were instrumental in causing this process of change to increase dramatically, and consciousness – *Oneness* – moves in the direction of evolving toward a life form capable of becoming aware of the subtle underlying reality that we call consciousness, and what I call, in this book: *Oneness*. So, that would be evolving stages until a brain and mind capable of becoming aware *that we are all one; that there is only a single entity (or source) from which all this grand symphony emanates/resonates.*

# Wake Up!

And even if the Earth was getting smaller or larger, it would be due to change – and only change... It would be going somewhere (changing from this to that), or coming from somewhere (changing from that to this).

Despite my effort to explain *Oneness,* and to help everyone to understand the delusion that is caused by the mind, and the minds trappings, many may still think: well then... ...after I die, then I will continue along as the *Oneness...* ...so will I be a tree, or a rock, or another human, an animal, a fish... ...what will I become?

Such an idea implies being separate again.

Another word and concept that might help for some people is the word 'Lifeforce.' We reduce Lifeforce to the individual aspect with the word and concept of *'soul.'* Soul is humanities conception of the individual Lifeforce.

There is only one Lifeforce, and that is *Oneness.* All that exists bubbles forth from *Oneness.* All things and all change that occur are bubbling forth from *Oneness.* You won't continue on as a tree or some other animal or object, because you already are *Oneness,* which is all you ever were to begin with. Just as I have said: "When I look around the room I see many different objects, and I know that I am that, and I am that, and I am that" – or as Hindu wisdom dictates: "be always the seer and never the seen." You already are all of those things – it's just that you (a mind) in a human body are not able to sense that you pervade all of the other spaces within the *Oneness* – and that's a good thing because it is very very HOT in the Sun, and I don't think you'd like to have any sense of

154

# The Dream of the Mind.

that while you are flesh and blood. Remember my analogy with the lights in your house... You are the electricity (*Oneness*) – not the objects that are plugged into the *Oneness* which come to life from the *Oneness*. You are not the body that you currently occupy – you are the *Oneness* that gives life to the flesh that you currently consider yourself to be. It would be better if I change the last phase to this: "you are the *Oneness* that gives life to the flesh that '*it*' occupies." Your separateness is relative. The first word in that phase, "you" is simply all of your experiences and memories that the body you see in the mirror has recorded in your brain as a story. Your intuition knows the *Oneness* which exists underneath all your memories and experience, but the mind wants the *Oneness* to be limited to all of your experiences and memories. The mind is deluded, it's a basketcase! It just won't give up! It is only your mind that causes the dichotomy – the split.

But then... ...You are *it,* and it is *you*! ...which again gives credence to the phrase: From the *Oneness* come many, yet the many are but *Oneness*.

Gives entirely new meaning to the phrase: "Be all that you can be."


I have quoted a couple of quantum physicists, Psychologist Carl Jung, Cultural Anthropologist Joseph Campbell, and a few others but it's important that I don't get overly tangential or nuanced. I feel like I'm already tangential and repetitive more than I would want. The mind always wants more, and in this case – explaining this – less is not just better, but necessary. I could have quoted tons of resources, a slough of websites, books and authors, but I didn't because – what's the point; giving you a tour of a rabbit hole with countless side tunnels would only make this a convoluted romp through mind vomit. The point is only this: Wake

# Wake Up!

Up to what you *really* are – not what you *relatively* are, but what you *really* are. We think we are so smart, but keep watching the show as we destroy ourselves. Our first order of business is to Wake Up, then we can go about being smart.

I've read so much I can't remember it all, and my personal narrative continues to grow, and new pages cover the old so that it gets hard to remember the last chapter, except that I know it's only a narrative – but if you call me by my name I will turn; my mind is useful – but it's just a tool, nothing more.

What I am talking about in these pages cannot be proven – it simply is, and I am, and I am that. I didn't become aware because of the Wizard of Oz story, or any other allegorical story, but they do help us greatly to understand.

I didn't start really seeing how prolific allegory was until after I Woke Up. After Waking Up I looked deeply into what resources are available, and all of it contributed to my ability to explain this in better terms, contemporaneous to our current era, of our deliberate and most often subconscious self-effort to wake ourselves from the dream of the mind, but my reading is not the *source* of what I now write; my reading has helped me to explain this, but it is not the source. The source of what I write came about due to a heightened awareness out of the gate, and then a tragedy, and a total meltdown in my identity which snapped me out of my distraction.

When I saw the delusion and convolution of the mind I began seeing all of the allegorical signposts that we have created both consciously and unconsciously to wake us up to this knowledge. I didn't read books to

# The Dream of the Mind.

awaken me; it was the inverse: I awoke and then read books to help me explain it.

I learned that my mind was a fiction due to a tragedy that liquidated the narrative of me, the narrative that had been created in my head, just as surely as Dorothy liquidated the wicked witch and thus assimilated all aspects of her. Then it immediately became apparent to me that there are countless signposts, they immediately were everywhere, and I recognized them for what they are; – *we have deliberately made ourselves a bread crumb trail leading us home to the truth of our being*, but for some reason, the bread crumb trail is elusive to almost everyone. I stepped through the looking-glass, and there is no turning back once that happens!

It has been my goal throughout these pages to reduce them to as few as possible. The mind always wants more tangentially, and I happen to know that it's imperative to not give the mind too much. The mind would rather wait for just a bit more information... The mind would rather you don't listen... "he's gotta give us some proof." The proof will never materialize... you have to wake up to it.

Have you ever heard that 'less is better' or that 'less is more'? Well, that's the case with becoming aware of the underlying truth of who and what you are. You are much simpler than all the clutter in your head, yet you are much more than you will ever be able to comprehend using all the clutter in your head – that you identify with. So, less is better. Reduce...reduce...reduce.

Learn to quiet your mind occasionally, but more importantly, *watch your mind vigilantly* – as in staying alert to its traps; keeping your awareness that your mind is useful as a tool, but otherwise a bunch of crap that will keep you churning in your feelings. Keep your mind under a watchful eye. It's funny: the mind watching the mind, but with the realization and understanding that the mind is a fictional narrative, it is possible – although, not always easy to do objectively and consistently. Remember to see everything as a part of yourself – entertain this concept even if you don't believe it. Everything you see, hear, and feel is all a part of you; try to be a part of it. It can be hard – your mind won't like some of the things that you come in contact with, especially of the human ilk, but this is all one big dance, and there is only one thing behind it all, and that thing pervades everything including you and is what gives you life, and what powers your body. Don't slip and think: "No, what I eat powers my body." Such would be another slip and down the hole you fall... because that which *'is'* – *Oneness* – pervades what you eat too. Everything is a vibration of and emanates from *Oneness*.

Do you remember what I said about every part of dream symbolism being an aspect of the dreamer? It's not just in the dream; in the physical world everything is an aspect of *Oneness* – all are part of the whole! The One becomes Many, yet the Many are but One.

Nothing... **NOTHING** is separate. Quit listening to your mind except as a tool. *Always the seer and never the seen.* See everything as yourself and respect what you see as you respect yourself. It's like the saying: Treat others as you would want them to treat you. This just goes one step further: Treat everything as you would like to be treated. That doesn't mean that you can't shoot a rabbit and eat it – or eat a carrot. That's how nature works – and nature is *Oneness*. Eventually, something will eat you. It's all one grand symphony of life happening, and things eat each other just as the maggots will eat your body and the bacteria will eat the maggot when the maggot dies, or after it changes into a fly – if a bird doesn't get it first. Wolves might eat you, or they might eat your friend – not good, not

# The Dream of the Mind.

bad, just is. And you don't go kill the wolves for eating your friend, or for eating your cattle – they're just being wolves. Remember always to love one another. I've often heard it said: It matters not what you do for yourself, but matters most what you do for others, but this is better said this way: *It matters **less** what you do for yourself, and **more** what you do for others.* ...because you first must take care of yourself before you can help others, and although that isn't *always* true – you do have to take care of yourself as well as helping others.

At the same time it is important to not do for others what they can do for themselves; for if you do, you are not helping them. Life is difficult and everyone must learn to do for themselves. For example: If you allow an old person to be sedentary because they are old, and you do everything for them, then you are doing them more harm than good – they need the exercise up to a certain extent; it takes careful discrimination to determine when it's time to get up and help them. Same with a child; If you treat them like an infant you will be holding them back – once they learn something, make them do it for themselves. If your child knows how to tie his/her shoe, then don't tie it for them. If they make a knot, help them get it out, but show them how to do it for themselves.

It can make me sad, and it can be depressing at times to watch the ugly things that happen in this world due to people's unwillingness to subdue their minds. These 'bad' things that happen are due to our identifying with our minds, and the real tragedy is that our minds are merely fiction. Ugh!!!

Please try to understand and see your mind as the narrative and fiction that it is! Our suffering is directly correlated to the degree that we identify with our mind. With that said, as long as you live you will need to allow your mind to exist, to some degree, in your head – no way around it, try to shut it off – can't be done. You would have to turn off the electrical field in your body and if you did that you would be dead! We all must be able to process thoughts that are necessary to survive. The key concept here is 'identity.' We needn't believe ourself to be that person that our mind would have us believe. At the same time, our community needs to identify us in the group so we need a name and skills to contribute, but these are only labels, and we needn't identify with them beyond that.

Our suffering is not only due to identifying with the mind as an individual, but our suffering is also directly correlated to the suffering we inflict on others – intentionally or unintentionally. Our mind is the origin of our ideas about others, beliefs about others, and the projections we make upon and about others. The reason that our suffering is not only due to identifying with the mind but is also correlated to the suffering we inflict on others is because 'there is only one' and to inflict suffering onto others means we are inflicting it on ourself.

If you identify with your mind you will see yourself as 'other' and miss the fact that we are one, and you cannot inflict any harm on anything anywhere without harming that which "is" – which is what you are. You may not see the effect of the turmoil, stress, or tension (the bad things) that you inject into the environment, but it goes out there... somewhere. But so does the love, compassion, and truth (the good things) that you inject into the environment – it goes out there somewhere. Sometimes you will see the direct results, and sometimes you will not. As I have pointed out: it's all vibrational.

At the same time, our strength and wisdom come from how well we suffer when we are confronted with suffering; how well we *endure* our

# The Dream of the Mind.

suffering.  To be stoic – stoicism.

I bounce back easier because I realize my mind is a fiction, and I threw the damn book away – well... it's still here in my head, but I don't give it much credence anymore.  I use it for what it's needed for.

It doesn't change things in a bad way to turn inward, nor does it make your life any more difficult to turn inward and discover that connectedness we all share.  It won't necessarily make you happier, but it gives you understanding – which can make you a little more stable and content with 'what is.'

I still feel hurt when I see others who are hurting or causing hurt.  I also suffer from frustration when I try to explain what's in these pages to someone and their eyebrows furrow, and their head tilts.  It's much easier for me to write it all out – that way I can take my time arranging the words for you.  Words can be monsters!

When I talk about this with someone extemporaneously I have a hard time arranging the words spontaneously to properly convey the concepts when talking to someone.  I have a fairly large vocabulary, but my brain can get stuck when I try to explain complex concepts *extemporaneously,* and if I hesitate in my sentence... the questions start flying, and my whole line of concentration and reasoning gets lost as though a gentle breeze blew it away.

The minds of others want to pick apart each concept, one at a time, which pulls the entire conversation into a circular pattern – and any mind can run a circular race because there is no end to a circular argument – which keeps the mind in control, but more importantly, as long as the mind searches for truth it will always be chasing the wind – for truth is relative in the physical realm, and with human beings, there is *always* another point of view.

Your mind will try to find fault whenever possible. Your mind wants the world to fit your mind's conception of *what 'is' **according to your mind***. Your mind is unable to resolve the mystical, but your mind thinks it can – so it will try, and it will try to convince you to trust it. So... it is much better if I write it all out – no questions or interruptions. I very much realize that I'm repetitive, but I think it's necessary.

Many people think that after you die you go to heaven that it's all joy and happiness. This is not the case. If there were a heaven and it was happy then at times it would also need to be sad – because one polarity cannot exist without the other. Same for hell, if hell were all unhappiness and misery then at times it would have to be sheer joy and pleasure. Understand that happiness and sadness are polarities, and these particular two (happiness and sadness) are *mind qualities* (mental qualities). They are not attributes that are intrinsic to that which 'is.' Mind qualities are endemic to animals with brains and therefore minds. The state of *Oneness*, if one could describe it in the very limited human terms available to us – it would be best described as contentment. Just content. Not happy, not sad, not depressed, not joyful, none of our human emotions will properly describe it. I think contentment is the best word available. It's content. But content has discontent as a polarity so even contentment isn't precise – but its the best word I can think of. Maybe 'equanimity' or 'balance' would be better...??? Words are so limiting and one person can read something one way and another person reads it to mean something altogether different; semantics. This is precisely why we use allegory and metaphor and why Jesus used parable to make a point.

# The Dream of the Mind.

*Oneness* witnesses our horrors and fears, our joy and our sorrow, it witnesses everything and stays content, or equal/balanced. It is only when the mind comes into play that the polarities become unbalanced.

*Oneness* has the intent for us to Wake Up so that we quit hurting ourself /each other. Notice I wrote 'ourself/each other' rather than "ourself *'or'* each other." I don't confuse the fact that *we are each other* – it is the same. Your natural state is that of *Oneness* – find your balance.

*Find your balance between using your mind, and identifying with it – in that place, you will find contentment.*

The Buddhists say find your bliss. And by bliss they mean contentment. Some people think that bliss is some ecstatic euphoria – not so; bliss is simply equanimity – balance. Joseph Campbell always said, "Follow your bliss."

Heaven is a mind thing (fictional place) invented by people who think they are better than others – that they deserve more just-deserts than individual's who have not been as productive, or as nice or kind, or who have not fit into ordered society, or who have hurt others, or who simply do not share in their cherished beliefs.

...and hell is the place that those people who consider themselves more worthy have invented where they consign the people they feel are not deserving. None of the criminals and delinquents have invented hell as a place they want to go. No... nobody is going to invent some horrific place to commit themselves. The heaven and hell that some people say are actual places that you go after you die were invented by those folks;

people who think that their version of the god story is correct and yours is wrong; people who think they are more righteous than others – they have invented both places to make the people they accuse of being less deserving afraid, and to make themselves feel better. Most people who think that they are better and more deserving aren't better or more deserving at all – in fact, most of them aren't even nice.

You create your heaven, or your hell, right here on this earth by what you think; by what happens in your mind. That's the truth. Heaven and hell are places that are in the physical, and they are right here and now – not in some individualized, compartmentalized afterlife that is an illusion – a dream of the mind – hubris.

This is why zealots burn people or subject them to the worst punishments and torture that human beings can imagine... ...because they want people who have offended their mind dream to suffer unimaginably – to experience the hell that the zealots imagined up in their minds. The hell that they are compelled to inflict on people... ...because they don't even trust their own religious beliefs – they are uncertain as to whether there is a hell after death, or even if their God exists, so they inflict their own ideas of hell on people here in the physical world, so to make certain in their mind that their victims suffer the worst hell they can imagine – just in case the biblical hell doesn't exist.

They have the most convicting need to inflict the most excruciating pain onto those they are persecuting because they are not confident of their own belief in hell – for they wouldn't need to inflict **any** pain on those they want punished if they were *certain* of a real hell – wouldn't need to because those people they seek to punish would be going to that – *believed in* – hell which is more agonizing and horrific than anything imaginable.

# The Dream of the Mind.

To – let's say – burn someone at the stake would be 10 minutes of reprieve from the tortures of the – far worse – biblical hell, and to give them any reprieve from the biblical hell would be depriving their believed in God of his sovereign judgment and punishment.  Burning them or torturing them in this life is a reprieve from that hell, so why not just kill them and send them **directly** to that damning torment.  It is their *lack of confidence* and *uncertainty* in their own faith that causes them to torture people before they kill them – so they stand there as the pious executioners in their charlatanism.  That is the most profound sort of coward!!!  Mind vomit...mind vomit...mind vomit!


We seem to think that it's good against evil, but we are back in the mind again when we think this.  There is only one thing and it is **not** in conflict with itself, or against something 'other.'  We project that idea – it's not real.

Phrases such as "Treat others as you want them to treat you," and "Judge not lest you will be judged" become crystal clear when we realize we are all *One*; then the implication of these phrases make perfect sense because if you consider us as *One*, and you treat others badly, then you are incidentally treating yourself badly because there is only *one* thing – if you are treating someone badly *it can't be helped* that you are also treating yourself badly.

And if you live in the awareness of *Oneness*, and then judge another, it becomes quite easy to see what this statement actually implies.  It simply says that if you judge someone else you are judging yourself because both the judge and the one being judged are *One* in the same.  *WE ARE ONE!* Being in the knowledge that we are all *One* puts these teachings into the correct context – the correct light, the context that they were *meant* to be understood in the first place.

But, we can't get there overnight. People need to Wake Up to the narrative we call the mind, or what some eastern mystics call the dream of the mind. The more who Wake Up the more who will follow – it has a snowball effect.

If you need to read more, then read Carl Jung's "Man and His Symbols." Jung is good at explaining how archetypal symbols operate to tell us things in our dreams as well as our waking life.

Also, learn to recognize the allegory that we create to lead us to the truth. Read Joseph Campbell's books, but keep this in mind with Joseph Campbell's books: the older his books are (the earlier they were written) the more exceptionally hard and tedious they can be to read. The older books tend to be more academic and tangential. In this book, I have tried to keep it simple as possible by using 'The Wizard of Oz' as my main example of allegory. We all know this tale quite well so it doesn't take cryptic deciphering to understand it.

There are countless allegories; "The Hare and the Tortoise" is an allegory, 'The Three Little Pigs' is another, but the allegories of transcendence are the most important and neither The Hare and the Tortoise, nor The Three Little Pigs are allegories of *transcendence*. They are allegories to teach us a more basic life lesson, and most all allegories try to point in that direction. They provide a lesson that is important to the path of living in this world.

One thing I have learned is that the more education someone has the less they seem to understand – the narrower their vision tends to get. Here is a quote from Joseph Campbell: "It's not an advantage to be

# The Dream of the Mind.

without a PhD, but it's an advantage not to have taken a PhD because of the things that they do to you to get you into the slot that they want you in."[29]

This is very true of graduate degrees. People who obtain graduate degrees spend a huge portion of their life not just getting into their box, but after they are in it they spend the rest of their life better shaping, defining, arranging, rearranging their particular expertise – their 'box.' The more they are able to sharpen the picture of what they have studied, and the more they can develop the field, the greater the accolades they receive from their peers, and the more prestige they are given. The ego eats accolades for breakfast. They are more likely to miss the wider picture because they spend their adult lives – or most of it – focusing on a localized field – a narrower picture. Humanitie's obsession with education, while noble and smart, has become a monster. Notice that I said noble and smart... education is a good thing, but it has become tortured in that most fields outside of the stem fields are becoming nuanced into meaninglessness.

If you are one of these folks then getting out of the box will likely be harder for you; you will need to surrender more, and give up more; giving things up is not easy to do. Surrender of what you hold most dear is practically impossible! Until a person is *firmly rooted* in the knowledge that the mind is a fiction – a narrative, that person is going to keep slipping back into the illusions, obsessions, addictions, compulsions, and fantasies of the mind. I will admit that there are occasionally people who obtain Masters and Doctorates who have one foot in their box, yet are careful to keep the other foot out – but such people are the exception, not the norm –

---

29    Joseph Campbell, The Hero's Journey: Joseph Campbell on His Life & Work

although, most think that they are the exception.

My mind is very active, but I am only the observer of my mind; you don't need to completely quit using your mind as eastern mysticism might *seem* to imply. In the Eastern mystic philosophies, they want to spend an inordinate amount of time in meditation, or in effort to separate themselves from thoughts and thinking. It's not a matter of quieting the mind in order to become aware. It is a very peaceful thing to not have ones mind constantly abuzz with noise, but it's more important that one does not *identify* with the mind, and with the narrative of who you think you are – which is a fiction. I no longer identify with my mind except for the purpose of participating in the world; I am not of this world though – if I spoke openly and honestly to people they would think that I'm out of my mind, and they would be quite correct. I try to always keep my words consistent with the truth of *Oneness* we all share, and if I am unable to incorporate it into my conversation, I simply remain kind, and/or say nothing at all. I don't mind being blunt and straightforward when it is necessary – even though it can get me in trouble. Although, first and foremost, I like to joke, and spoof, and make people laugh.

Being caught in the *Dream of the Mind* is a pretty bad predicament to be in, so making a joke of it – if you understand that it's an illusion, and you're not taking it seriously – can be a good thing. Being that I am aware that my mind is nothing more than a narrative (not being caught up in the Dream of the Mind), and being the observer rather than the subject, I could probably be more successful in life – more focused on things, but my mind is very restless and I stumble in my focus (get tripped up by the Dream of the Mind, which has a great deal to do with why I have to write this all out rather than explain it to people extemporaneously), but that doesn't mean that I cannot remember that all the restlessness in my mind –

# The Dream of the Mind.

all of the mind vomit is anything other than mind vomit... I always know that my mind is simply a meandering compilation of thoughts that one day will end, and mean nothing. I am not my thoughts, nor am I the culmination of my experience. I am, and I am that, and that, and that.


There is an image in Buddhist philosophy that shows the mind as an out-of-control elephant with several Buddhist monks wrestling the elephant down – subduing it. This is a good image. The mind is like that elephant out-of-control. The Buddhist might meditate to help control that out-of-control elephant, but you can't meditate all the time. Quieting your mind is a good exercise, but what is the more important thing is to simply not identify with that elephant. You can watch as it runs amok and not run amok with it. It's just an elephant running amok!

We are so caught up in 'me me' syndrome – especially in the West. The East has me me me problems, but they also have a better understanding of 'us.' Eastern mysticism teaches the 'us' philosophy. In the West, Christianity does teach to "do unto others as you would have them do unto you" and "love one another...," and "don't judge your neighbor," etc., but the West puts those ideas beneath the idea that you will go to heaven simply by asking for forgiveness from God, accepting Jesus as your personal Savior, being baptized, etc.

There are differences in the Christian ideology denominationally, but it enables the Christian to 'live as a sinner as long as that Christian has accepted Jesus Christ as his/her Lord and Savior.' The Christian can't avoid the "sinner" identity because it is one of those facts like 'the Earth is flat' fact. And as sinners, they can transgress and still go to heaven if they accept Jesus as Lord and Savior, and repent. Can you see how this allows

169

the Christian to stay in his/her own circular trap? Giving oneself permission to stay in The Dream of the Mind. Instead of incorporating the Shadow they reject it and are forgiven for succumbing to it. Theirs is a very insidious paradox.

So... on this entire planet, all people have the freedom (free will) to live in the dream of the mind. A false place that is but a narrative – and in the bigger picture, putting all our personal narratives together to make a collective tome.

Allegory is our road map. We receive it more accurately while sleeping, but are better at delineating its meaning during waking hours. We should use it purposefully, yet we don't use it very well – if we use it at all, and then most people don't recognize it when it's there. The most important allegory is the personal allegory that is most often the product of a dream. Most allegories come to us in the form of stories from books and movies, and we can use these third party allegories to guide us, but the personal allegory (a dream) speaks to you directly.

As I pointed out: sometimes people who create these allegories are conscious of what they are trying to say in the allegory, but more often people write about the transcendent state in allegorical form without realizing fully what it is they are conveying – they sense it, and write it down, but don't fully understand it, and the message can get skewed, and not properly structured, delineated, and/or articulated. They know they are writing a clever story, but don't realize its import, and when they don't know the import they can accidentally mix the elements incorrectly, or perhaps leave important elements out. That's why so many stories, such as Avatar, are great stories but fail to hit the transcendent nail on the head.

# The Dream of the Mind.

Consider all I have said here - that you are *One* with all things, and that the individual only applies to us being different bodies walking around in the world, but that underneath the disguise of the flesh we are all *One*, and that our mind is the obstacle to recognizing this.

Consider what I have said that if all of us were to recognize our *Oneness* and act accordingly, then all this mayhem would slowly start to go away. The pendulum would slow, and then start to swing back. So... my point is that if this is true, then our fall from grace – our identification with the mind – would then be recognized as having been no more than mental illness, despite the fact that we – in our mental illness – don't define identifying with the mind (our mental illness) with mental illness. But, who in their right mind would want all the mayhem we collectively collaborate to create.

The mental neuroses that we see, all the addiction and addictive behavior, OCD, and other neurotic behavior that we experience in our communities is only from non-awareness: *identification with the narrative.* This isn't saying that if you are *not* suffering from what our psychologists have identified as a neurosis that you must therefore be aligned with *Oneness.* Quite contrary... ...almost every single person lives in the dream of the mind even though they seem, and are seen, as mentally normal by societal standards. In actuality, the exact opposite is closer to the truth.

Within the field of psychology there is a mental disorder called *"Dissociative Identity Disorder,"* but it's all backward and inside out. My primary axiom is that our lives are a narrative which is a fiction, and I have called it: "The Dream of the Mind." But... by societal standards (from within the Dream of the Mind), dissociative identity disorder means that someone living in our collective dream is not **properly** 'grounded' in their particular character role within the narrative within that dream.

But what I am telling you is that Dissociative Identity Disorder is identifying with one's personal narrative to *any* degree... living in the Dream of the Mind – Period! You don't need to identify with your narrative, nor with the collective narrative – on any level. The reality is that the "dissociative condition" is the current state of mind of almost every single human on this planet. When mental disorders are apparent they exist always in the mind. Many people have allowed their mind to make too real the heaven and hell that we have created, and that we serve up in movies and story-line, and in our everyday lives.

Many times I have seen teachings that speak about things such as wellness and the correlation wellness has with a healthy mind. There are problems that happen in the brain such as chemical imbalances, tumors, small strokes, etc., physical maladies.

...but the only true *mental* illness is identification with the mind. A mind has no health. Either you are aware that the mind is a cognitive space where you can float the memories stored in your brain so you can form thoughts and make decisions, or you think that your mind is who you are. If you think that your mind is who you are then you are trapped as the character of the narrative, a fictional story – you *identify with your mind, (have dissociative identity disorder)*, and thus you become the end product of your imaginings.

If you identify with the mind then you will try to win admiration from those around you; you will want to be recognized as the character of your personal narrative, for your accomplishments and your possessions; you will want others to love you, or at minimum, to respect you. You will be a

# The Dream of the Mind.

self preservationist instead of a self sacrificer. You have become the victim of your mind, and, ...if you are not successful in the world, or not getting what you think you need, then you will suffer depression, frustration, or some other neurotic symptom(s) that will manifest in all sorts of ways as what some call mental illness, but the only 'mental illness' is your *identity* as the aggregate of all your experiences, feelings, beliefs, and inculcation from your parents, teachers, friends, TV, and social media, etc. The only true 'mental illness' is identifying with the mind – the personal narrative, a fictional story.

Whereas, if you are aware of the mind as a spectre, a narrative, a story that is relative only to life experience, then you will only need the mind as a tool for survival, and to help others to become aware; you will love all, and won't care if others love you or not. Aware humans have a history of ending up on a spike. It's not that they are not loved, just that they are loved only by the few people who can understand them, and loathed by those who live in the dream of the mind, those who can't understand them; those who cling to fanatical mind vomit systems to retain power, material possessions, and life everlasting promises they get from their religious beliefs. Most everyone identifies with the mind, and they have a distaste for those who have transcended the mind. Aware people don't say the right things to them – aware people are not interested in placating anyone's ego. People who identify with their mind see aware people as out of their mind crazy... ...because people who identify with their mind haven't even the slightest hint of *Oneness*.

I find it interesting as I talk about this that the words, however elegantly they are coming to me, or however carefully I arrange them, they keep failing to convey, ***with unblemished accuracy***, the truth behind what is being conveyed. ...words... ugh!

Think about what I have been saying: "that we are a unified whole." So, when someone else (an **other** – *which they are not*) tells you they don't love you, they are misidentifying with their mind as an individual separate from you. In the true sense, it is their mind that doesn't like your mind. Not that they don't love you, they just don't like your mind, or perhaps their mind doesn't like the body that has manifested into this world that is labeled with whatever you have for a name, and the experiences that you identify with as being the essence of who you are – which is yet another misidentification.

I often tell people: "I love everybody," but when I'm among strangers I might couch it in a phrase such as: "Something's gotta be wrong with me because I love everyone." When I say it this way people smile because if you love everyone then something must be wrong with you, so I give them a tiny way to rationalize something that *most* people think is idiotic or absurd.

Most people – and particularly those people who are in positions of power – believe that changing things to the degree that I am suggesting can't, and never will, happen. Well, what I am saying in this book is real, and that we have **no choice** (no alternative) but to return to being *One*, and until we do, things will continue to deteriorate until we do exactly what those in power are saying we can't do, which is jettison all of this mind vomit except for what is needed for living in the physical world. We are the ones who created this delusion we suffer from, so.... as organic goop bubbling up from *Oneness*, we cannot help but collect our karmic consequences in each and every step if we don't correct things because we are just one thing inflicting harm onto itself by inflicting it on others – which are not 'other.' So... we just drop poop on our own head. Mind vomit manifests!


Either way, we have to scale back dramatically - if we don't then our own subconscious (*Oneness*) will see that it happens anyway through some catastrophe or perhaps a simple virus. If we don't do it smartly, we will do it stupidly – because deep within us, intuitively (Oneness), we know it must happen one way or the other. Karmic consequences don't come from a source separate from us. Karmic consequences are those consequences that in our minds we have assigned to ourselves as punishment for not doing what intuitively we know is just and right. We will experience those consequences that we have assigned to our ethos. What we think, so we become! *All feelings become manifest.*

If we go the way of the dream of the mind (our fictional narrative) we destroy ourselves, and whatever few humans survive will have to rebuild while remaining in the dream of the mind which is a vicious circle, but if we Wake Up to our *Oneness,* and live together always understanding *Oneness,* keeping the focus that we are all one, and we systematically make decisions to scale back by attrition those things we know are harming us, and our planet, and thus move forward, then we will deny the mind its dreams of individuality, and we will be okay. Things will slowly balance out. The pendulum will always swing back. We can keep those parts of our technology that are useful yet not pollute, or harm *ourself in the form of the Earth – which is part of us.* It's going to be one way or the other; we learn how to control our minds, or our minds continue to control us and destroy us, and we continue to live inside a dream and continue to experience mind vomit.    The Earth does not live in the Dream, so therefore we are diametrically opposed to the intent and will of nature. There is nothing wrong with thinking deeply, but being deeply identified with the mind is another matter altogether.  You use your mind, or your mind uses you – those are the only two options.  You are either a *human being* **that which 'is'** *(Oneness)*, or you are a *human **doing*** **things that are separate** from *Oneness*, that are merely part of your narrative – individual or collective.

I have said that the mind would happily destroy everything in its effort to control things and that after it had destroyed everything that all that would be left is *Oneness* – thus the mind would have merely destroyed itself.  The mind cannot win.  The pundits and high priests will say we can't change to the effect that I have suggested.   Well, what these ideologues and high priests suggest is a contradiction, you could even call it a perceptual paradox because the ideologues and high priests live in the dream of the mind, and therefore their ideas and thoughts *are the mind trying to continue along – the mind trying to stay in control – the mind insisting to us that  we can't exist unless we agree with the dream of the mind – preaching on high from the pulpit of delusion.*

Since the mind can't possibly win, the mind dreamers can't win.  They are the 'awareness sleeping' – an oxymoron.  All humans are potential awareness/not yet aware  –  living the dream of the mind: *potential awareness (asleep in a dream).*

Our aligning ourselves with the dream of the mind, the narrative, and believing ourselves to be separate is metaphorically what Christians call the Antichrist.  The biblical "Antichrist" is quite plainly the archetype of the individual.   The Antichrist will take control and ruin humanity.

# The Dream of the Mind.

Christian scholars characterize the Antichrist as the Devil. Well... it sort-of is in an allegorical sense. The Antichrist will come into power and lead the world into destruction. Absolutely! If we stay in the individual, if we remain lost in the Dream of the Mind, it will bring us to destruction.

Christ – in the Christian allegory, – is the metaphor that represents salvation that brings us back into union with *Oneness*, and Anti-Christ is Anti-*Oneness* – which is individuality. The Antichrist is simply our false identity with our mind which is a refusal to see and become attuned with our true nature – *Oneness*. Christ is metaphorically the reunion, Eden was the separation from God (*Oneness*), and Christ is the denouement to that story, and metaphorically brings us full circle to the resurrection (reunion) from the death of the Eden allegory. Death belongs to identity with form: *an individual separate from Oneness.*

People can't see these metaphors, and I am sometimes astonished that they can't pick them out as easily as I do. Even the erudite theologians can't see them. I couldn't recognize them until my identity vaporized so... I do understand that if people don't see the mind as a false self, and they are unable to understand what the mind is... then I can see how they fail to understand.

Our body and everything associated with it, and attributed to it is the temporary thing. All of the temporary is lost when we die – yet none of it is really lost because none of it is permanent in the first place and is subject to **change** in this dance of the physical universe. Nothing in the physical is permanent; the ONLY thing that is permanent is the *Oneness*, and that's all you are, and all that you ever were – so, No Worries!

Of course, there are mediums, and those who proclaim to see ghosts, but they do so for the money it makes for them, or the notoriety that it brings to them, both of which are power in different forms.

The mind will forever find ways to convince us that we are individuals with individual souls. The mind is an electrical field that connects all of the memories in our brain and allows instantaneous recall which allows us to compile this narrative that we call [your name], and our identity with it (ego) is obsessed with continuing forever. The human mind will find every possible angle to intertwine into every transcendent allegory and metaphor a twist to the story that perpetuates the individual narrative through the concept of an individual soul, and when our path brings us close to the truth, the mind will find a new twist to that path that again perpetuates the narrative. Even the Eden allegory and the Wizard of Oz allegory have previously been explained incorrectly. With every allegory, someone seems to come up with some tortured version of what it should mean in order to sustain an agenda. Then there are people who will tell us stories of ghosts, spectres, and spirits, because our minds are already obsessed with continuing along, and we are susceptible to these deceptions. This is what I was emphasizing earlier – making that final leap is practically impossible which is why 'faith' is often cited as the only way to get there. You have to be willing to make the jump, and not worry about the fall (the death of the false self), which requires *faith*. The warrior walks into battle and dies a good death.

Oneness doesn't need and isn't interested in existing any other way than that way it already, and always has existed. It simply 'is,' and you simply are one with it, and that's the end of the story. When your body wears out, that which 'is' will continue along as that which you have always been. You are not your body. You are not the narrative that is your experience. Quit the attachment to it! No worries! The warrior walks into battle and dies a good death. No worries! Use your body for

# The Dream of the Mind.

good things while you have it, but quit identifying with it. You don't need an individual soul unless you want to stay in the *Dream of the Mind* – the personal narrative you have created which corresponds to your experiences – the false story of the individual which will bring you nothing but grief and aggravation – your own little heaven **and** hell.

To even think that you are this person that you have become over the past however many years you have been alive is – essentially – just some short-sighted mental illness. The Dream of the Mind begins the narrative at birth and ends when the narrative ends at death. Live in the truth of that which is: The Dream of the Mind begins where One becomes Many, and ends where the Many are but One.

So... you might think that there is no point in being good because you don't go to heaven after your body wears out and dies, nor do you end up in hell after your body wears out and dies; you simply end up where you always were in the first place, so your mind might try to trick you – once again – by saying to you, what's the point? ...no reason to be naughty or nice.

That's backward thinking from the start. You create your own heaven or hell right here on this earth by what you think – by what happens in your mind, which governs your behavior – which governs your outcome. It is only by creating your own contentment here that you benefit while living in the physical world. You don't have to worry about what happens after your body dies, but you should do everything in your power to do good in this life here in the physical realm, and help others to find contentment as well. To live in awareness is to live in love, and to help others around you to do the same.

Contentment comes from your doing your best to be kindhearted, loving, generous, etc. Being mean, or a thug, or a degenerate only brings aggravation and stress to you and to others. You must become aware of who and what you really are because when you do that... the rest will happen automatically – all by itself, you won't have to try because *you simply 'are.'*

*Oneness* bubbles up (manifests) as the physical world, and the intent is to become aware of *Oneness*, and aligned with *Oneness* while in physical form. When that happens *Oneness* and contentment will become your reality in the physical realm. ...doesn't mean you won't have problems, but you will no longer identify with your problems as part of who and what you are.

Thinking that you will not live eternally as this identity you believe yourself to be doesn't mean you don't go on forever – it only means you don't go on forever as this *narrative* you believe yourself to be. If you Wake Up to who and what you really are then you do go on forever because you make the correct association with what you really are: that which 'is.' Let me say that in different words: If you Wake Up to who and what you really are you no longer consider yourself as the continuing narrative of [your name] after your body dies – you simply are, and continue to be that which you simply are, and always have been. The continuation of [your name] implies the narrative, and the narrative is the delusion/fiction.

You needn't worry about the state of the underlying reality, or what we think of as afterlife. What you have to focus on is the physical realm and what happens here – that's our purpose and – essentially – our assignment while in the physical body. To bring awareness (bliss) into the physical realm. To Wake Up!

# The Dream of the Mind.

We (all that 'is') keeps bubbling forth from the underlying (the *logos*) into the physical, and we need to bring our awareness of it into this physical side of what is. To do that we must be awake to it.

Don't worry about death, dying and decay. That all takes care of itself. Without "mind" all of the death and decay simply recycle back to the elements that nourish the living. They ***change***. Then they change more, and the bubbling forth just goes round and round. Nothing bad in that – it just 'is.' Remember this: *Living is far more difficult than dying and death.*


So... now... if you understand that, let's talk about what many of you already know: ***What you put into your head, so you become***. This isn't so hard to understand or to believe because we have heard it before in this form, and also in other ways of saying the same thing, such as: what you believe so you become, or what you believe you manifest into your life, or what you wish for you just might get, sort of like the idea of prayer, or concentrating and focusing on something so much that it becomes your reality. As you believe, so you shall receive. These concepts are true, but the best way to think of it is simply that what you put into your narrative, so you become that.

Who you are now, and what you believe yourself to be, is simply the aggregate and culmination of what you have written into your narrative – how you have constructed the self you believe yourself to be. I have not said that you cannot have your narrative. You must have a narrative to survive in the physical world – you must have a mind and its resulting concomitant story.

I'm only saying that you mustn't identify with your narrative.

# Wake Up!

If suddenly you had amnesia and couldn't remember anything, and you had none of the people around you that knew you before, you could rewrite your narrative from that point forward, and actually **be** that new person. So... do you understand? You are not who or what you think. 'Mind' and 'Think' are synonymous. Your mind is the only thing that thinks, and the resulting narrative that your mind conceptualizes, compiles, and stores in the cells of your brain, is not who or what you are. Your brain does not think – it stores your thoughts, that then become what we call memories. See your mind for the spectre that it is, and then it cannot trick you anymore.


I'm not a fan of religion in the non-mystical sense, and particularly Christianity, Islam, and Judaism, yet in their mystical underpinnings they are all legitimate paths to the same underlying *mystical* truth: that we are all very much connected – very much *Oneness*. I have used quite a bit of the biblical road map in my explanations, but I'm not a Christian, or any other religious follower.

We must love one another. When we control our mind rather than the mind controlling us – then loving one another becomes natural, and then the rest comes together by itself. We won't have to stop polluting the earth because we simply won't pollute any more, because we are the earth, we are the water, we are the air, we are each others brother/sister – in fact, we are each other. Nothing is actually separate. "I am," or "I am that," or as Hindu mystics have said: "Be always the seer and never the seen." To not be seen removes the individual from the equation. You look out upon the world and see only your self – you see only the seer.

The point I want to make by pointing to and explaining allegory is that

# The Dream of the Mind.

the road map is everywhere, and has always been there for us, we are constantly holding this mirror up and trying to get ourself to see this very basic truth – but we keep coming up short. I can't prove any of this. None of those people who have presented this information before me using other terms have been able to *prove* it – and many people have tried. It cannot be proven, and it cannot be explained through conversation because conversation always becomes tangential – that is the very reason it is explained through allegory – if it could be proven everyone would be aware already. Mysticism is that which cannot be put into words... the mystery... that which cannot be explained but can only be experienced.

Truly amazing to me is listening to certain people talk about it... ...they dance around it and often hit the nail smack on the head, but each time they slip back into the quicksand of *The Dream of the Mind.*

Having read this; knowing this, raises the bar for you. You are more responsible now. For example, if I had not written this book knowing what I know, then I would have neglected my responsibility to you. Go buy the Wizard of Oz and watch it now – except, explain it to your children correctly – they deserve that! There are many allegories that you might use, but I've helped you understand The Wizard of Oz allegory, so it will be the easiest for you to use. They may not understand it right off, but your practiced *Oneness* nurtures and fosters theirs.

Ultimately, if we continue to live in the dream of the mind, the joke is on us because *Oneness* is all there is. The truth of what we are: 'One Single Thing' content to the highest degree, blows away any of the myriad utopian schemes of heaven and/or individualized, compartmentalized utopian euphoria conceptualized by the mind. It is inevitable that *Oneness* will continue to create the vibration that spawns creation, and that eventually an intelligent form of life will arise that will not just have the awareness of the underlying *Oneness*, but will live in that Oneness. It's also inevitable that humanity will suffer intolerably from our own folly if we continue to identify with our mind and allow our mind to control the moment – to reject *Oneness* (symbolized metaphorically as God), in lieu of our mind, the individual (symbolized metaphorically as the Antichrist). That is the lesson in the Garden of Eden (before the Jesus denouement), that we have free will, and will suffer death. It's time to move into the denouement and be reborn into the awareness of our true essence, our true nature, our underlying reality: *Oneness* – "I am."

*Oneness* has the last laugh – so to speak – because we will continue to go through this until *Oneness* gets what it intends: to live in the physical world with full awareness of *Oneness* in all beings at all times. That which underlies all of what we see as reality and the physical world (*Oneness*), is *'still'* – calm beyond anything we can imagine, patient beyond our conception of patience. *Oneness* is in equanimity, and will remain in equanimity, because there is no waiting for *Oneness* – there is only *now*. . . Eternity.

There are some sayings: "Everyone is entitled to their opinion," "To each his own," etc., there are many of these little cliches.' These cliches can be misleading. Many cliches are "enablers." They give people a rationale, and thereby the justification, to do as they please – "free will" to live in the dream of the mind, to live in ones own delusion, and spread delusion to others.

To live in one's opinion – is to live in one's mind – which is The Dream of the Mind – the personal narrative. Once upon a time there was an opinion that the world was flat. There were others who believed the world was a sphere which was considered another opinion, except it wasn't an opinion, *it is _fact_*.

People can and will say that this book is an "opinion," but I will tell you outright – expressly – that what is in this book isn't an opinion, it is fact. I don't "think" it is a fact, nor do I "believe" it to be fact. "Thinking" and "believing" are things of the mind. I *know* that what is written here is fact because it is my experience. I am! This is what Jesus, Krishna, Buddha, and all of the sages have wanted us to understand. They taught for the times in which they lived, using the tools of language and science that were available during their time periods – My message is for the present time – which is **Now.** This book is the only guidance I will provide – it is complete in content to what you need to Wake Up.

I realize that to make the assertion that I know this to be fact is one of those things that people frown upon, but regardless, I assert this proposition as a fact and not theory.

# In the End...

My only concern is:

# Wake Up!

And this is all happening now. Either we Wake Up and take care of each other, and our planet, or we continue to create our own heaven and hell due to the dream of the individual who we identify with. The Dream of the Mind, and the Dream of the Individual is the same. The Mind is where the Individual resides.

If we destroy ourselves things don't really come to an end as some might like to think.  Big change for *humans*, but everything else will just go on with hardly a hiccup.  Everything continues along.  Life is unfolding, bubbling forth from *Oneness*, the vibration, every moment.

Ten billion years is only a single moment – no time is lost as the mind would like to us to think.  If organic life doesn't happen here, it is happening elsewhere.  We can destroy ourse<u>lves</u> (multiplicity – the many), but we will never be able to destroy ourse<u>lf</u> (*Oneness*).  *Oneness* isn't losing much by losing humans, but we are completely lost without the awareness of that which 'is.'  What you think, so you become!  So start thinking correctly.

THE ONE HAS BECOME MANY, YET THE MANY ARE BUT ONE.  We are to become aware while in our bodies; we are to Wake Up!

*That, ...my brothers and sisters...   ...is the whole idea!*

Made in the USA
Middletown, DE
05 October 2020

21154627R00104